ENCOUNTERS

The 1999 Methodist Companion

Encounters
Published by Methodist Publishing House
© Trustees Methodist Church Purposes, 1998

Compiled by Susan Hibbins
Illustrations © Steven Hall

Printed in Great Britain by Stanley Hunt Limited

ISBN 1 85852 106 8

CONTENTS

FOREWORD

Here is a rich variety of ways in which men and women have encountered God. This book shows how different human beings are and how diverse are the ways which God had of touching their lives. For some their encounter was through the created world, for others it was through people or events or an inward experience. The people through whom God influenced them were also varied – a peasant woman, a youth club leader, a doctor, a minister expounding the Bible.

Most of us are fascinated by what happens to other people, and yet the fascination is not just curiosity. Reading what happened to others and how they responded to it is interesting and challenging in itself, but it also enlarges our vision and understanding. Others help us to see the world and people with their eyes and not just our own. For me – and no doubt for you – the writers' testimony was a stimulus to think, not only about their story, but also about encounters in the Bible and in my own life.

We could describe the Bible as the story of encounter with God – or perhaps rather of God's encounter with us. You have only to think of Adam and Eve in the garden, Abraham and Isaac on Mount Moriah, and Jacob at Bethel – and you are still only part way through the first book of the Bible. After that you turn over the pages and read of dozens of others – of Moses by the burning bush, Elijah on Mount Carmel, and Isaiah in the temple.

In the Bible some of the encounters are ordinary, others extraordinary; some are in a holy place, others in a desert; some are a meeting with people, others a meeting with God almost face to face. There is also an astonishing variety in the time and place and manner of the meeting. In some cases people hide from God, in others they are searching for him – but in all the encounters there is the possibility of a new stage in the person's life.

The book made me also look afresh at encounters in my own life. I thought of those moments – worshipping in church, walking on the cliffs, skiing in the mountains – when I had an overwhelming sense of the presence of God. I recalled those occasions when he challenged me through friends or books or films – changing my view of life or its direction, encouraging me in sorrow or bereavement, opening my eyes to the needs and hopes and fears of others. But these testimonies also made me wonder how often God has encountered me in his world or in other people, and I did not recognise him – and how often I did not let the encounter change me. For an encounter is never just a point of arrival, it is also a point of departure.

I hope this book will encourage and stimulate you. I commend it to you.

Peter Stephens
President of the Methodist Conference, 1998-99

CREATION

*For the Lord your God is bringing you into a
good land, with springs and underground waters
welling up in valleys and hills, a land of wheat
and barley, of vines and fig trees and pomegranates,
a land of olive trees and honey.*

Deuteronomy 8:7-8

Much Marvelling in the Marsh

Jack Burton

13th February: At the close of an early shift I made a dash for the marsh. I was tired and I was busy – yet I went. 'Why?' I asked myself. Yet I knew the answer. I went because I needed to go. Inwardly I felt drained and empty. My heart and my flesh cried out for the living God: for communion with the earth and sky, for unity, for healing . . . As I walked along the path through the trees that fringe the marsh, my footsteps crunched in the snow. I stopped and listened. The trees held their bare arms around me; the tension and stress fell away. 'Hello!' I whispered quietly, 'I have come . . .'

Having spent thirty years of unorthodox ministry working as a bus driver, I ought to be writing about involvement in the daily life of the world: about meeting God in the labours and suffering, the loves and laughter, of men and women. Instead I want to share my rest-day experiences – encounters which are doubly precious since, by recharging my batteries in secret, they help to make possible the robust public witness which is sustained only by long periods of quietness and reflection. If Jesus had the hills, I have the marsh.

My marsh is part of a recently-designated National Nature Reserve, and only a twenty-five minute bus-ride away. It combines grazing marshes, vast reed beds, pools and dykes, a tidal river and stretches of damp woodland. It lies beneath wide skies, and is bathed in that peculiarly clear light, characteristic of the region and beloved of artists. I can be found at the marsh, usually with my wife, whenever opportunity permits; but I prefer not to be found! I revel in the solitude and the spaciousness. They restore my soul.

I am not a wildlife expert, a twitcher, or a scientist, though I can identify many species by name. Merely being there is enough, consciously part of the life of the marsh – if only for a few hours – and allowing whatever is happening around me to happen also within me. Dying in autumn, rising again in spring, to me the marsh is about getting in touch, simply and undramatically, with the vital life of our living planet. It is about tending something we have neglected, affirming something we have denied, restoring something we have removed, and finding something we have lost. Just by being there; simply by melting into the reeds and alders.

The marsh presents an endless variety of faces. It is always the same, yet different, its atmosphere constantly changing. Different times of the day affect its appearance. So do the ever-changing seasons, the weather, the cloud and the light. But – to use religious terminology – it never fails to bestow its blessing. It possesses a strange ability to heal, sustain and renew. Even wet days are exciting, for without rain there would be no marsh to enjoy.

In winter the marsh can be cruel, yet I have many precious winter memories. There are calm, restful days, neither too hot nor too cold, when inquisitive robins and scolding wrens remain on duty, and great crested grebes make farmyard noises out on the river, but little else stirs. I like these times of apparent inactivity, when nature seems still to be resting and recovering, content to wait, survive, and prepare for the days of frenzied activity which will come soon enough.

Particularly invigorating are the clear bright days when – despite the ice lingering on the puddles – the creatures pretend that spring is already here! Starlings whistle, tits chase one another, woodpeckers laugh and call and drum furiously on their favourite branches. Flocks of wigeon twist and turn above the grazing marsh, their plumage spectacular as it catches the light, and large formations of wild geese pass overhead.

But on the marsh the harshest winter days are not for the faint-hearted. When the wind carves beautifully-curved snow-sculptures in the lane, or when the dykes are frozen hard, it's tempting to remain at home. When wind-chill makes minus four degrees feel like minus sixteen, it's hard to believe that venturing out will be worth the effort.

Yet even on the cruellest days, surprise encounters are possible. One February morning, with visibility reduced by driving snow, I watched a forlorn pair of bearded tits, just a few feet away, and a harrier appeared suddenly above the reeds, closer – again – than ever I'd seen one before. After the snow, the sunshine reveals a landscape transfigured and glorified. Tracks can be followed in the snow, while a little blood-stained circle of feathers marks where a sparrowhawk has taken a fieldfare.

Spring comes to the marsh in a series of subtle changes and exciting discoveries. The elements of the earth are infused with new life which activates their dormant energy. The whole world becomes vibrant and tender with promise. Then I long for that same renewing power to rise in me, and make all things new. Signs of the awakening appear on every side. Snowdrops in the wood; frogs and toads in the dykes; crocuses in the marshman's garden; catkins on the hazel and alder. The geese and wigeon fly north; the afternoons lengthen; coltsfoot flowers beside the path. And suddenly, what has been approaching hour by hour is there in all its passion and abandon. It is a heady cocktail.

Lapwings tumble in crazed aerial antics; snipe drum their tail feathers as they hurtle earthward; a cacophony of raucous sound envelops the rookery. There is new warmth in the sun. Although some days remain cold and wet, the marsh seems to smile. In the woods, amid every green shade imaginable, are celandines, primroses and bluebells. New sounds are heard as migrants return: chiffchaff, willow-warbler, blackcap.

On the grazing marsh, a distant spot of gold can be either a yellow wagtail or a clump of marsh-marigolds. Departing fieldfares are replaced by brazen sedge-warblers, shy reed-warblers and trilling grasshopper-warblers. The hares turn mad, stoats patrol stealthily, cuckoos call monotonously, and marsh-harriers exchange sticks in high-altitude courtship rituals. 'What is all this juice and all this joy?' Spring is when the lid comes off and exhilaration overflows. 'The voice of the turtle is heard in our land' – and many other voices too, especially in the great dawn chorus.

The tempo quickens. There follow days of swallows and swifts and martins; of brimstone butterflies, orange-tips and holly-blues, of forget-me-nots, lady's smock and cow-parsley, of sunshine and billowy clouds creating patterns of light and shade across the reeds. (Incidentally, sunset over the reedbeds is an experience unlike any other, when the last blazing rays light up the feathery reed-heads, and any drops of moisture hanging there glisten like diamonds.) Wild ducks are always in the sky; yellow flags bedeck the ditches; swans, coots, moorhens and grebes perch for days on nests of reed, then proudly parade their young. The gull colony maintains an unendurable volume of quarrelsome noise, and rare swallow-tail butterflies flap over the reeds like small, beautiful birds.

As spring melts into summer, the scent of honeysuckle fills the wood each evening, and day by day the temperature soars out on the marsh. Then is its true glory revealed – for this marsh has never been ploughed or sprayed with herbicides. In consequence, it flowers with an abundance seldom seen today: marsh orchids, spotted orchids, yellow rattle, meadow vetchling, ragged-robin, meadowsweet, yellow loosestrife, purple loosestrife, both of the tall willowherbs, marsh-pea, meadow-rue, hemp-agrimony, marsh-thistle and very many more. Goldfinches feed on the seed-heads; grasshoppers, dragonflies and damselflies are everywhere, with peacock butterflies, gatekeepers and meadow-browns. However, for enjoying this summer beauty there is a price to be paid! Determined and vicious insects inflict bites which often hurt at the time, and turn to swellings which last for days. Yet even these can't keep me away.

High summer can seem strangely quiet on the marsh. All the frenzy is over, and there is a lull, a sense of stillness and serenity as the cattle graze and, just for a short time, nothing seems to be at stake. It doesn't last long! Autumn, with its mists and colours, its first frosts and its shortening days, provides a sharp, passionate stimulus no other season can equal. Each year, its melancholy appeal threatens to break my heart. And as the summer visitors pass through and depart, the first winter visitors arrive – the noisy northern thrushes, then the wigeon and the geese ...

The peace of the marsh is never more powerful than in autumn. Sometimes the unutterable beauty of the season makes it very difficult for me to come away. I linger even as darkness falls, sniffing the scent of rotting leaves, glad that here, at least, I belong. When birds and small rustling creatures hurry away I murmur: 'It's all right! It's only me. It's only Jack!'

31st December: Then, in deep twilight, I waited among the shadows, eager and alert, staring intently first at the marsh, then across the field to the church tower. 'Come on! Come out of the church, old barn owl!' I ordered. I scanned the marsh again, without success. I repeated my command a second, then a third time. A thrill of excitement and fulfilment swept over me as, in the darkness, I discerned a white, mysterious form floating across the marsh. The silent shape passed close, and a heart-shaped face turned toward me. It was an acknowledgement, a recognition, a benediction on the year, and a promise . . .

Our God is the God of all people,
the God of heaven and earth,
the God of sea, of river, of sun and moon and
    stars,
of the lofty mountains and the lowly valleys.
The God above heaven,
The God under heaven,
The God in heaven.
He has his dwelling round heaven,
and earth and sea, and all that is in them.
He inspires all,
He quickens all,
He dominates all,
He sustains all.

                        St Patrick

It is this sense of mystery – unfading, because the veil is never lifted – that gives glory to the countryside, tenderness to atmosphere. It is this that sends one man to the wilds, another to dig a garden, that inspires the pagan to build an altar and the child to make a cowslip ball. For in each of us is implanted the capacity for loving his fellow and nature and the Creator of them. These loves may be latent, but they are there.

                        Mary Webb

At a Quaker meeting recently I was feeding my faith by thinking of God as I had seen him in natural beauty. Memory is a strange thing! The most vivid of all were memories of childhood – the wide stretch of shining wet sand set with little sunlit pools when we went down to bathe before breakfast on summer mornings, when the air was full of salt-sweetness.

A walk along the cliffs through cornfields on a wonderful summer afternoon of radiant sunshine, when the sky was vividly blue . . . the marvel of an Easter sunset reflected in Lake Windermere.

My work keeps me now nearly always in dirty, paved streets and under smoky skies, but I came away on Sunday refreshed as by a day in the country, and with my thoughts of God re-splendoured.

Source unknown

It may have been only a thorn bush that Moses saw that day, a thorn bush ablaze with blossom, or a tree in the flaming colours of autumn, or the sun shining on a patch of vegetation. But God made it the means of revelation; [Moses] felt that he was on holy ground, and listened for what God had to say.

Francis B. James

Leaving the patchwork forests
We entered the cathedral:
High-domed arches green and gold
Beneath the vaulted heavens,
Branches meeting and embracing overhead,
Our footfalls hushed on a carpet of bronze gold
Stretching away ahead along the aisles.
Feathery larches, bronze-fringed green,
Dressed in wedding finery; here and there
Triumphant gold branches pointed heavenward,
    sounding
A fanfare to their Maker. As we trod
Between the bare pillars of leafless trees, we saw
Others attired in vestments of celebration red,
And a million leaves like copper and gold coins,
Largesse shaken out with a liberal hand.
This was holy ground, for ever along our path
We encountered burning bushes, signs of
    your presence,
And we took off our shoes and worshipped.

                             Rosemary Lindsay

Thou art the Breath
That stirs the forest trees;
Thou art the mystic Silence
   Of the hills;
Thou art the Light
That floods all lands and sea;
Thou, O my Lord,
Art Light and Life to me.

Anonymous

The trees are singing my music, or am I singing theirs?

Edward Elgar, speaking of *The Dream of Gerontius*

We need to find God, and he cannot be found in noise
and restlessness. See how nature – trees, flowers, grass
– grows in silence. The more we receive in prayer the
more we can give in the active life. We need silence to
be able to touch souls. The essential thing is not what
we say, but what God says through us.

Mother Teresa

It was very early in the morning as I walked with my friend, the farmer, across the rich dark fenland. The sun was rising and flooding the fields with light. Our spirits rose and some strange light within scattered the dark problems we had been facing the night before. We did not see their solution yet, but we saw how small they were, for as we paused for a moment at a stile it seemed that God himself was with us. The immensity of our difficulties shrank into littleness; we were in the very presence of God.

Leslie F. Church

God of the hills, grant me your strength to go back to the cities without faltering – strength to do my daily task without tiring and with enthusiasm; strength to help my neighbour who has no hills to remember.

God of the stars, may I take back the gift of friendship, of love for all. Fill me with a great tenderness for the needy person at every turning.

God of the wilderness, with the harsh winds of winter drive away my selfishness and hypocrisy. Fill me with the breadth and depth and the height of the wilderness, and may I live out the truth which you have taught me, by every thought and word and deed.

Irene Mott

Fat Ada and the Growing Edge of Trees

Celia Haddon

Where were you, God, when I needed you? I know that I do not have a very good channel of communication with you at the best of times, but where were you when I was sliding into the pit of despair? For I am one of those people who suffers from depression, and in my darkest hours God has been absent or present only as a condemning, angry judge.

It was one morning eight years ago that I sat on the side of my bed as I dressed for work, and looked at my husband, Ronnie. My mind seemed completely clear. The world seemed a beautiful place, only marred by a filthy blot which was me. Ronnie will be much happier without me, I thought. He will be relieved of this disgusting person who blights his life. I have no right to exist. The very thought of me made me want to shudder.

At this point God was not there. Definitely absent. My saviour came in the shape of my overweight black and white cat, Fat Ada. I looked at Fat Ada, an immensely neurotic cat, and the thought arose that she too would be happier without me. Then it occurred to me that perhaps she wouldn't be. As she didn't really love any other human being except for me, she needed me. The slender thread of her happiness bound me to life.

Those who have not suffered from depression often think that it is like ordinary gloom or unhappiness. It is much, much worse. The pain of one's thoughts is so acute, the landscape of the mind so utterly without redemption, that it is difficult to find words to express it. My self-loathing was so great I could not look at myself in a mirror or a photograph without turning away in disgust.

God was no help to me at first. Indeed, at times his absence was preferable to his presence. He was potentially part of the darkness. I remember one dreadful day with particular horror. It was a day when I woke up convinced that I was doomed to hell, utterly outcast from any hope of God's mercy, as disgusting to his eyes as to my own.

Nor was the figure of Jesus Christ helpful that day or later. When I thought about Jesus, I thought of the tortured body on the cross. There were days when I felt the pain of every wretched stray dog or dying London pigeon, and on days like these I dared not think of Jesus at all. The idea that I should follow him seemed to suggest that my life should also be full of pain, that happiness would be a shameful betrayal.

God and Jesus did not help at those times, but therapy did. In counselling sessions, I recalled the time when I had been told, by a Catholic nurse, that I would burn in hell forever because I had not (at the age of five) been baptised. I had pictured myself dying outcast from God's mercy. My childish fear and distress had come back to haunt me in later life. I understood it, which gave me the weapons to push it away.

I was writing a book of quotations and some of them were woven into my recovery. The day when I felt I was doomed to eternal torture, I caught hold of this: 'For thou lovest all the things that are, and abhorrest nothing which thou hast made.' I said it over and over again to myself till the gaping mouth of hell retreated by the end of the day. I drowned out the doom by repetition.

'God didn't bring us so far, to throw us away,' was one sentence which comforted. Cardinal Newman's reminder that 'I have my mission – I may never know it in this life, but I shall be told it in the next' – helped me realise that there was a reason for going on living, though it felt as if there wasn't. Later I came across Henry Vaughan's words: 'Be pleased to remember that there are bright stars under the most palpable clouds, and light is never so beautiful as in the presence of darkness.' And many others. People who offered kindness helped. People who offered solutions did not. I learned to be careful what I told to whom. And slowly God came back a little. I would go into empty churches and just cry. My prayer was simply, 'I am here, God.' Nothing else.

I learned to be careful about God though. If the God of condemnation came back into my mind, I simply turned away from God for a bit. Better no God at all, than that God. That God might well kill me. I continued going to church, but made a conscious effort not to listen to the bits that distressed me. I skipped the Good Friday service, so that I wouldn't feel the tortured pain of the occasion seeping into my being. I had enough pain to bear without that.

I started a new way of praying. I lay flat on my back, and simply saw myself as a child walking towards a source of light and love. I imagined myself being blessed by it. I let go the ritual of thinking about sins or asking for help. I thought how much I loved Fat Ada, and how her neurotic behaviour made me love her more, not less. Maybe God felt about me as I felt about her.

I began to be able to notice the beauty of the world, without feeling that I was not entitled to be a part of it. There were strange moments of joy. I saw a red fire engine racing through the streets and I felt its beauty deep in my heart. Someone used the phrase 'the growing edge of trees', and I would look up at the trees and see their tracery against the sky. When I lay on the grass I thought of 'the delighted insects' described by the poet John Clare, another sufferer from depression.

I was coming back to self-love. My pain wasn't wasted. It gave a kind of depth to my life, and, after all, I survived. Some people don't. I have a photograph of myself and another girl taken in 1968. She killed herself and I couldn't help her in her suffering because I hadn't been there. Now I can sometimes help others a little.

There is a temptation to lie and say my depression gave me great religious insights. It didn't. It did, however, teach me emotional honesty towards God.

Now I won't go through the motions of praise or thanksgiving when I don't feel like it. That is behaviour which you have to fake for a tyrant, not for a friend. I trust him enough to tell him that I don't trust him. When I am angry with him, I tell him so. For weeks after Fat Ada died, I railed at him about the unfairness of cutting her life short.

Did depression bring me closer to God? No. I am not very near him and I often think maybe he doesn't exist anyway. Yet I also think these opinions of mine simply do not matter. My little mental and emotional reactions are not, after all, important. I aim to try less and let go more. Somewhere is a sort of trust in the divine ingenuity.

After all, his love got through to me – by means of a fat black and white cat, the growing edge of trees, a reform Jewish therapist with a taste for dangling earrings, and daily encounters with kind humans, charming beasts and beautiful plants. As Jacob Bauthumley wrote:

> God is in all creatures, man and beast, fish and fowl, and every green thing from the highest cedar to the ivy on the wall; and that God is the life and being of them all.

For me, I am nearest to him through them.

Father, we praise thee, now the night is over;
Active and watchful, stand we all before thee;
Singing we offer prayer and meditation:
Thus we adore thee.

Monarch of all things, fit us for thy mansions;
Banish our weakness, health and wholeness sending;
Bring us to heaven, where thy saints united
Joy without ending.

All holy Father, Son and equal Spirit,
Trinity blessèd, send us thy salvation:
Thine is the glory, gleaming and resounding
Through all creation.

Gregory the Great

15th May 1759: I rode over to Lorton, a little village at the foot of a high mountain. Many came from a considerable distance, and I believe did not repent of their labour, for they found God to be a God both of the hills and valleys, and nowhere more present than in the mountains of Cumberland.

John Wesley

How can you buy or sell the sky, the warmth of the land? The idea is strange to us. If we do not own the freshness of the air and the sparkle of the water, how can you buy them? Every part of this Earth is sacred to my people. Every shining pine needle, every sandy shore, every mist in the dark woods, every clearing and humming insect is holy in the memory and experience of my people . . . We are part of the Earth and it is part of us. The perfumed flowers are our sisters; the deer, the horse, the great eagle, these are our brothers. The rocky crests, the juices in the meadows, the body heat of the pony, and man – all belong to the same family.

If you sell our land, love it as we've loved it. Care for it as we've cared for it. And with all your strength, with all your might, and with all your heart preserve it for your children, and love it as God loves us all. One thing we know – our God is the same God. This earth is precious to him.

> Chief Seattle, in reply to the US President who in 1850 requested the Native Americans to sell their lands and move to a reservation.

Great Spirit,
still brooding over the world –

We see the cry of the earth,
We see the sorrow of land
raped and plundered in our greed
for its varied resources.

We hear the cry of the waters,
we see the sorrow of stream and ocean
polluted by the poisons
we release into them.

We hear the cry of the animals,
we see the sorrow of bird, fish and beast
needlessly suffering and dying
to serve our profit or sport or vanity.

Please teach us

> a proper sensitivity
> towards your feeling creation
> a proper simplicity
> in the way we live in our environment
> a proper appreciation
> of the connectedness of all things
> a proper respect
> for the shalom of the universe.

We turn from our arrogant ways to seek you again,
Lord of all life. Redeem us – and redeem your world
and heal its wounds and dry its tears. May our
response to you bear fruit in a fresh sense of
responsibility towards everything you have created.

Kate Compston

Breathe in praise of your Creator
Every soul his honours raise
Magnify the Lord of nature
Magnify the God of grace
Hallelujah,
Fill the universe with praise!

Charles Wesley

Go out alone on the hills and listen. You will hear much. The winds will hold you for you will hear something more than sound; the stream will not be merely the babbling of hurrying water. The trees and flowers are not so separate from you as they are at other times, but very near; the same substances, the same rhythm, the same song binds you to them. Alone amidst Nature, a person learns to be one with all, and all with One.

Frank S. Smythe

I feel immersed in God like a drop in the ocean, like a star in the immensity of night; like a lark in the summer sun or a fish in the sea.

Carlo Caretto

It may indeed be only fantasy
That I essay to draw from all created things,
Deep, heartfelt, inward joy that closely clings
And finds in leaves and flowers that round me lie
Lessons of love and earnest piety.
So let it be – and though the whole world rings
In mock of this belief; to me it brings
Nor fear, nor grief, nor vain perplexity.
So will I rear my altar in the fields
And the blue sky my fretted dome shall be;
And the sweet fragrance that the wild flower
    yields
Shall be the incense that I offer thee –
Thee, only God, and thou will not despise
Even me, the priest of this poor sacrifice.

S. T. Coleridge

The Lake of Galilee is, of all the places that I have seen, the one in which the Spirit of Christ is still present. There is only lake water falling on black stones, a slow procession of crops, the ripening of fruit, the bright flight of the kingfisher and bee-catcher, the sun by day and the stars by night. Time has taken no revenge on the lakeside where Christianity was born. In the silence of the night the little fishing boats set off under the stars as they used to when a Voice called from the shore: 'Come after me, and I will make you fishers of men.'

H. V. Morton

Moments of Joy

Susan Smith

When I was very young, I lived with my family in a house which had a large garden. As well as two lawns, there was a rockery and a trellis over which climbed a wild rose, and golden rod and Michaelmas daisies flowered every year. But alongside the flower-beds on the left of the garden was a secret path, shaded by trees and plants, that was always rather dark and quiet, not sinister but strangely mysterious. I often used to play there, pretending I was in a jungle, or that I was one of Robin Hood's merry men, creeping through Sherwood Forest. When the wind blew, the trees whispered together, and I used to try and catch what they were saying, but I was never quite able to.

One memory of that time has stayed with me, though, for nearly forty years. Sunshine was dappling through the leaves, shifting and swaying as the trees moved in the breeze, and suddenly I was aware of a presence with me, though I saw nothing and heard no-one speak. I only knew that it was a 'good' presence, not frightening but full of joy. It was like a memory of something I had known before, an echo of something, some other happiness that seemed familiar and was yet new.

Now when I look back on this experience – and it must have made a lasting impression on me to stay so vivid in my mind – I chart it as my first awareness of God's presence, even though I was too young to recognise it as such. But I have been blessed since then to be given many such fleeting 'moments', always full of joy, and always in contemplation of some part of God's creation.

William Blake once said that some people are moved by the beauty of a tree, while others see it merely as a green thing that stands in their way. God gives us much to enjoy in the world, much in creation that can comfort us in times of difficulty or sorrow, but it is easy to take it for granted and become unaware of the sights and sounds that are scattered in our path. My heart can be warmed and lifted to praise by the sound of the dawn chorus in spring, by the sight of a million stars on a frosty winter's night, by the sound of rain falling on thirsty summer leaves.

The sky is another great gift, constantly changing, especially as the Divine artist tries out a new sunset design every night. Living close to the Lincolnshire fens as I do, and missing the hills of my home county of Derbyshire, I find some compensation in the huge fenland skies and uninterrupted sunsets. People and buildings are dwarfed in comparison, and sometimes it seems that they could easily be crushed by the vastness overhead.

There is also in creation a mighty power, which makes me think of God's greatness. Much is made today of God's gentleness towards his children, of his care and concern for us, and it is right that we should see him as a loving Parent. But we must not forget his greatness and his majesty, and we should stand in awe of both. I am reminded of the majesty of God in great storms of thunder and lightning, in gales and in the power of the waves of the sea. Cornwall is a favourite holiday destination for my husband and me, and though naturally we hope for good weather while we are there, we are glad if we have one stormy day with high winds and crashing seas. There is something exhilarating about a rough sea – watching it or sailing on it.

But like all bad weather, the power of the sea can be destructive. Even in our own country extreme weather can bring danger with it. Sometimes it seems that our reliance on technology and on machines in every aspect of our lives – helpful though those things are – has created the illusion that we are in total control of the world and everything in it; and yet it takes only a few feet of snow to bring transport to a standstill, demolish our power cables and leave our computer screens blank.

I read recently that scientists had detected in the universe a burst of energy so great that the 'echo' of it had taken sixteen billion light years to reach us. The event had thus taken place before the creation of the earth. It is information like this which makes us feel puny, small and insignificant, and perhaps it is right that it should. The miracle is that the God who sustains such a universe also creates each individual snowflake, and numbers the hairs of our heads.

Thinking of the universe in this way also causes me to remember that, despite outward appearances, the creation that we look on is not a permanent thing. Changes take place constantly, stars are born and die, and scientists are still only able to guess at the history of the few planets we are able to study.

The same is true of our own tiny world. In Deuteronomy, Moses blesses the Israelites, and to Joseph he says:

> Blessed by the Lord be his land,
> with the choice gifts of heaven above,
> and of the deep that lies beneath;
> with the choice fruits of the sun,
> and the rich yield of the months;
> with the finest produce of the ancient mountains,
> and the abundance of the everlasting hills . . .

> Deuteronomy 33:13-15

To us, as to the Israelites, no doubt the hills do seem 'everlasting'. Day follows night, and the seasons succeed one another, year after year. In a world where the pace of change can be bewildering, we revisit scenes of our childhood and are glad to see that they are still familiar. We may lose our loved ones, but we can look on the beauty of the world that God has given us, thank him and find comfort in our sorrow. Human beings have probably always felt that their world would last for ever; Britain once had an Empire 'on which the sun never set'.

But such permanence, as we know, is an illusion. The 'ancient mountains' may once have been at the bottom of the sea. The countries in which we live may have begun as parts of other land masses many thousands of miles from where they are now, and they are still changing year by year. The earth is constantly on the move. And, sad to say, it is slowly being spoiled by the very people who are meant to be its stewards. It is only God who is permanent, it is only he who is changeless, and only in him can we find real joy and lasting reassurance.

And yet we can still find him in those 'moments of joy' which he gives us in creation. In his poem 'God's Grandeur', Gerard Manley Hopkins bemoans the fact that human beings have lost touch with the earth that God has made, in their preoccupation with 'trade' and 'toil'. The 'grandeur' is lost, or worse, ignored. But, he concludes:

> . . . for all this, nature is never spent;
> There lives the dearest freshness deep down things;
> And though the last lights off the black West went
> Oh, morning, at the brown brink eastward, springs –
> Because the Holy Ghost over the bent
> World broods with warm breast and with ah!
>   bright wings.

The whole universe makes a statement about its Creator. The pattern of the coming of light and dark, the changing seasons, the rhythm of birth and death and new life – the never-ending cycle of creation – in all of this we can see, if we are willing, the handiwork of God. There is nothing more powerful than the sun, and the daily rising of the sun has always been something which early people acknowledged with respect. This is something we sophisticated, modern, often urbane people should learn from. We should never take for granted this daily gift of God to us. Although we live with the assumption that the sun will rise daily, we should never allow ourselves to take this daily miracle for granted.

Esther de Waal

I went out alone, and I hardly know how I shall say what befell. A glorious wind was blowing in from the west across the Irish Sea, driving along with it warm, thin rain. As I faced it my soul suddenly leaped forth. I felt what a cramped-up, stuffy life the life of my soul had often been, and I shouted against the wind, yes, shouted in prayer to the God of that wind to blow the rushing west wind of his spirit into mine, and make it as healthful and free and blowy as that gale from the sea.

The Story of Temple Gardiner

O Earth! thou hast not any wind that blows
   Which is not music; every weed of thine
   Pressed rightly flows in aromatic wine;
And every humble hedgerow flower that grows,
   And every little brown bird that doth sing,
Hath something greater than itself, and bears
   A living word to every living thing,
Albeit it holds the message unawares.
All shapes and sounds have something which
      is not
   Of them: a Spirit broods among the grass;
Vague outlines of the Everlasting Thought
   Lie in the melting shadows as they pass;
   The touch of an Eternal Presence thrills
   The fringes of the sunsets and the hills.

                  Richard Realf

This is God's world, and it is a world which he is creating, not just a world he has created.

                  D. T. Niles

When you look at the smallest flower blooming this minute in the hedgerows, say to yourself: 'God made *that.*' When you see an absurd hen strutting about as though she owned the farmyard, say: 'God made that funny thing.' We know he made the planets: we are always told, when we want to realise our own insignificance, to look at the heavens; but we are seldom told to look at the little familiar, lovely and amusing things that God also made, and so we get a one-sided idea of him.

Margaret Harwood

A bee amongst the flowers in spring is one of the cheerfullest objects that can be looked upon.

Archdeacon Paley

Ralph Vaughan Williams, when a boy, asked his mother what the arguments about *The Origin of Species* meant. She replied, 'The Bible says that God made the world in six days. Great Uncle Charles thinks it took longer, but we need not worry about it, for it is equally wonderful either way.'

Anonymous

I believe in God's World,
In beauty of earth and sky and sea;
In sunbeams playing on rippling water;
In moon and stars milking the midnight sky;
I believe in God's World.

I believe in God's World,
In green life pulsing through brown earth,
In miracle of bud and flower and fruit;
In great trees raising gnarled arms 'gainst
    rain and wind;
I believe in God's World.

I believe in God's World,
In cry of new-born seeking the life-giving breast;
In gnarled old-age dozing in the sun;
In sweating brown backs bent over the
    unyielding soil;
I believe in God's World.

I believe in God's World,
In daily toil for daily bread,
In hurry and rush to factory, shop and mill,
In cries of the hungry, half-asleep, half-filled,
I believe in God's World.

I believe in God's World,
In the God-Man hung 'twixt earth and sky,
In the giving of one's life in the service of
    brother man,
I believe in God's World.

Gillian Rose

For two hours I walked alone and prayed: but pray as I would, I could not get one step nearer God all these seven or eight miles. My guilty conscience mocked me to my face. For two hours I struggled on, forsaken of God, and met neither God nor man all that chill afternoon. When, at last standing still and looking at the mountains clothed in white from top to bottom, this thought shot up into my heart: 'Wash me, and I shall be whiter than snow.' In a moment I was with God. Or rather, God, as I believe, was with me. Till I walked home, under the rising moon with my heart in a flame of prayer.

Alexander Whyte

There is a special responsibility laid on those of us who bring up our children in towns. The idea of God as Creator is not so easily passed on when much of our environment is man-made and unlovely. The sight of a strawberry to a child does not call up the memory of the silvery dew on the leaves, the feel of gossamer on the cheek, and the curly wispy mist of early morning. It is more likely to remind him of shops and money, 'punnets' and chips, and mother saying they are expensive.

Frances Wilkinson

The Himalayas

Alison Stedman

The morning light
brings them alive
And they awake
In the golden browns and greens
    that adorn them by day.
Frost nestling in the valleys,
A scattering of snow
Gathered in the crevices,
– whiteness blending
With the clouds that shroud the tops from view.
These distant, majestic peaks
Shout to the world,
Pointing heavenward
    to their Creator –
You, who chiselled the mountains from the earth
And raised them up
To cut across the sky,
Towering above us
    in awesome splendour –
They reflect your majesty.
As the sun sets,
The soft orange glow
Accentuates those craggy peaks,
And the dark shadow
Creeps down into the valley –
Until the blackness covers them –
Until the next morning
When they will
Shout again!

PEOPLE

For you are a people holy to the Lord your God;
the Lord your God has chosen you to be his people,
his treasured possession.

Deuteronomy 7:6

Tenacity, the Dragon Slayer

Ann Widdecombe

Public service is a vocation. People often forget that when they ask me how on earth I can mix Christianity with politics as if they were somehow incompatible as fire and water. Yet it is Christianity which informs my political convictions and those of every other Christian active in British public life. Of course we may arrive at different answers but there is nothing particularly odd about that: the various denominations of Christianity arrive at different answers and have been doing so for centuries.

'Let he that hath two coats give unto him that hath none.' I take that to be an exhortation to individual responsibility but my fellow Christians across the floor interpret the same text as justification for confiscating the second coat via taxation. No party has a monopoly of Christian virtue and we do well to remember that.

Of course Christians do not compromise and politicians do. Ministers speak as Ministers and not as individuals and therefore they will sometimes defend policies in which they have only very limited personal confidence.   Without the basis of collective responsibility government would become unworkable. It is therefore a considerable blessing that those issues on which no compromise would be possible – abortion, hanging, divorce, homosexuality, age of consent – are always decided by free votes.

Often when defending a supposedly hard-line policy I meet the allegation, 'Oh, you can't be a Christian if you do things like that!' Yet those who toss such a judgement around so lightly never pause to consider that those who make decisions have access to a great deal of information which is confidential to an individual citizen and which cannot properly be put into the public domain. It all comes down to trust, and sadly people are no longer so ready to trust their politicians.

This is not a situation we should be prepared to tolerate. Respect for our institutions is essential if democracy is to flourish and it should alarm every conscientious politician that he is now more likely to be distrusted than not, merely on the basis of the position he occupies. People have always muttered about politicians' promises but in the past they have done so with a nudge and a wink, not as now with a contemptuous sneer and utter conviction.

Yet politicians are as mixed as the people they represent. A few are stupid and a few are seriously dishonest, but to tar all with the same brush is to demean the vocational essence of public life. Many politicians embrace huge reductions in salary – which affect their families, not just themselves – in order to enter public service. They may well be politically ambitious but I never heard anyone decry nursing because an auxiliary aspired to be matron, or the priesthood because a vicar wanted to be a bishop. Yet it is almost *de rigeur* to condemn political ambition as intrinsically undesirable. This has always seemed to me grossly illogical, because presumably if you believe in something enough you will want to be in a position to bring it about. So I am ambitious, and that is not a fact which will ever feature in my visits to the confessional because ambition is merely one of the tools of achievement.

I am often asked if I am guided by answer to prayer and I say yes. The secular press love to present that as my believing that every controversial decision I take is part of a Divine mission but I make no such claim. I do sometimes wonder if Paul had the British tabloids in mind when he talked about the virtue of being long-suffering!

Many of my parliamentary prayers are directed straight to the Holy Spirit, the source of inspiration and wisdom. The nuns at my convent school always urged us to pray to the Holy Spirit before exams and the habit has stuck (although there was one exam before which I was advised to pray to St Jude instead, he being the patron saint of hopeless cases).

Mainly, however, politics is a game of patience in which you work on the same cause for years. The prize is to the persistent and enduring who never give up; it took William Wilberforce forty years to abolish slavery. When I suffer setbacks in the causes for which I am fighting I remember with gratitude the prayer of Francis Drake:

> O Lord God, when thou givest to
> thy servants to endeavour any great
> matter, grant us also to know that it
> is not the beginning, but the
> continuing of the same, until it be
> thoroughly finished, which yieldeth
> the true glory.

From early childhood, when I used to sing it at school my favourite hymn has been 'Father, hear the prayer we offer, not for ease that prayer shall be . . . but the steep and rugged pathway may we tread rejoicingly.' It goes on to talk of endeavour, failure and danger as the business of our life. In an age where comfort, quick-fix solutions and something for nothing are the order of the day it is unfashionable to preach self-restraint and endurance, let alone to suggest that it is actually the next life which matters, not this one. I have occasionally tried an approximation of this message on the doorstep but I cannot say it has been greeted with universal enthusiasm.

Endurance is taught in Holy Writ in a number of places but I always take particular comfort in the parable of the importunate widow (Luke 18:1-9) any time I think I may be boring heaven.

There are some people who are so close to God that you feel him near in their presence. Mother Teresa was one of those people and so is the Pope. Both have pursued long hard roads of dedicated service. Both set out to conquer something so vast it must have seemed impossible, both took a number of risks, and both have been accused of intolerance and of having authoritarian approaches. Both have responded by relying simply on the will of God. Karol Wojtyla has lived long enough to see the end of Communism, whereas Mother Teresa did not see the end of poverty in her lifetime, but neither has been short of determination, ambition and sheer bloody-minded tenacity. Nothing wrong with that – even in a politician.

I have always held to the principle that if you look for God you find God, and if you look for the devil you find the devil. It is not, however, only in manifestly holy people that we encounter God. He appears in some horribly unattractive people too. That is more difficult to remember, though it should not be, given what a ghastly lot the Apostles were. Peter was a foul-mouthed liar, Philip the most awful snob ('Can any good come out of Galilee?'), James and John vainglorious (arguing over who would be greatest in the kingdom of heaven), Thomas would not believe anything the others told him even though they spoke the truth, and Paul was a bigot who thought it quite in order to kill those with a different view. From this unpromising material Christ forged his church. Looking round the House of Commons at Question Time, I often think of the Apostles. It gives me hope.

'I was a stranger, and ye took me in: naked, and ye clothed me: I was sick, and ye visited me: I was in prison, and ye came unto me' (Matthew 25:35-6). That last statement was often in my mind when I was visiting all one hundred and thirty-five of Her Majesty's Prisons. I developed a special respect for the work of the Chaplains and Visitors who themselves faced a daily test of endurance as the same people came back inside time after time, nullifying the immense amount of work put in by prison officers, teachers, instructors and probation officers.

Were I the fairy godmother of the old-fashioned fairy tales I would not bother with the traditional gifts of beauty, riches or a handsome prince. I would give tenacity every time. In the end it slays dragons.

Help us to help each other, Lord,
Each other's cross to bear,
Let each his friendly aid afford,
And feel each other's care.

Help us to build each other up,
Our little stock improve;
Increase our faith, confirm our hope,
And perfect us in love.

Charles Wesley
(adapted)

To all who are weary and seek rest; to all who mourn and long for comfort; to all who struggle and desire victory; to all who sin and need a Saviour; to all who are idle and look for service; to all who are strangers and want fellowship; to all who hunger and thirst after righteousness; and to whomsoever will come – this church opens wide her doors and offers her welcome in the name of Jesus Christ her Lord.

The City Temple Church, London

'We mustn't question the ways of Providence,' said the Rector. 'Providence?' said the old woman, 'Don't talk to me about Providence. I've had enough of Providence. First he took my husband, and then he took my taters, but there's one above as'll teach him to mind his manners, if he doesn't look out!'
The Rector was much too distressed to challenge this remarkable piece of theology.

Dorothy L. Sayers

God gave to us the gift of coming naturally to him with our sorrows and our thanksgivings, as a child comes to a loving parent. A friend of mine told me of the occasion when he took his four year old granddaughter out with him. They had a wonderful day together. They went to the Zoo and Madame Tussaud's. They rode on the top of a bus. They had two meals out in restaurants. At the end of a magnificent day the tired and blissful little girl said her prayers, and told God all that she had seen and done and said. The prayer went on for over half an hour. At the end of it, no doubt conscious of its unusual length, she said, 'Well, that is rather a lot to remember, Lord, so here are the headlines again.'

Edward Rogers

Lord, use my hands; they are not scarred like thine,
  They have not felt the torture of the cross:
But they would know upon their palms
  Thy touch, without which all their work is loss.

Lord, use my hands, that some may see, not me,
  But thy divine compassion there expressed,
And know thy peace, and feel thy calm and rest.

                    A Fijian nurse's prayer

A Christian is full of love to his neighbour, of universal love; not confined to one sect or party; not restrained to those who agree with him in opinions, in outward modes of worship; or to those who are allied to him by blood or recommended by nearness of place. Neither does he love those only that love him or are endeared to him by intimacy of acquaintance. But his love resembles that of him, whose mercy is over all his works. It soars above all these scanty bounds, embracing neighbours and strangers, friends, enemies.

John Wesley

Jeremiah's Yoke

John Job

The year was 594 BCE. Three years earlier, in the middle of March, the city of Jerusalem had fallen after a brief siege to the troops of Nebuchadnezzar, ruler of Babylon. King Jehoiachin and the queen mother together with most of the people of any standing or ability were taken away in exile to Babylonia. Among them went the only other person whose name we know, the prophet Ezekiel. It was not Babylonian policy to impose direct rule on outlying provinces, so it was Jehoiachin's uncle, Zedekiah, who was made a puppet king. We must sympathise with him somewhat, since the taxation burden to finance the Babylonian empire and its active army might have made any government quail.

At any rate, after three years, Nebuchadnezzar ran into trouble. Contingents in the Akkad garrison, at the heart of his kingdom, attempted a coup, and as we learn from the clay tablets Nebuchadnezzar authorised to tell the tale (now in the British Museum), not only did he have many rebels executed, but killed the ringleader with his own hand. The Fertile Crescent may not have been as efficient as the Internet, but it functioned well as a swift means of communication. Probably Nebuchadnezzar's problem was much more serious than the version he committed to posterity suggests, and news of this upset soon reached

Jerusalem. Our story starts when envoys from neighbouring states came to Jerusalem for a conference to discuss with Zedekiah, while Nebuchadnezzar was thus embarrassed, a rising against Babylonian rule.

Jeremiah was against it.

Nor was it just at this particular juncture that he opposed military resistance to Babylon. It had been his unremitting message over the decade since Nebuchadnezzar's victory on the fords of the Euphrates at Carchemish changed the face of ancient history. Jeremiah had two reasons for making his stand. One was that, possibly from a much earlier treaty, but certainly from the time when Jehoiachin's father Jehoiakim had settled with Babylon, Judah was duty-bound to keep its side of the covenant. Nebuchadnezzar might have been harsh and the tribute tough, but a pact was a pact and it needed to be respected. It is a truth which is still relevant today, as we shall see.

The other reason was that the Babylonians were immensely strong. Of course, so had also been the Assyrian Sennacherib a century before when he attacked Jerusalem, as Jeremiah's contemporaries remembered, constantly harping on the invulnerability (as they naively believed) of Yahweh's temple abode. But in that situation, trembling Hezekiah had had right on his side, and that explained everything.

So when these ambassadors came from Edom, Moab, Ammon, Tyre and Sidon, Jeremiah was told to take a pair of yoke-pegs and attach them as a collar round his neck with cords. The equivalents of radio, television and the press were all in favour of taking a hard line with Babylon, and of encouraging the idea that the exile would soon be over. Jeremiah's yoke-pegs were a sign that this policy would only lead to further disaster.

The main group of opponents targeted by Jeremiah were those who have been called the 'optimistic prophets', and it was one of these, called Hananiah, who was party to the encounter we are concerned with. One day, after he had himself made a prophecy in the Temple that within two years the Babylonian menace would have evaporated, he met Jeremiah still wearing his yoke-pegs: he snatched the collar from his neck and smashed the wooden parts, announcing as he did so to the assembled populace that Yahweh would so break the yoke of Nebuchadnezzar in the short time he had forecast. Jeremiah did not react, but later he returned to Hananiah on Yahweh's instructions and told him that since he had broken the yoke-pegs of wood, they would be replaced by a yoke of iron, and that for preaching rebellion against Yahweh, Hananiah would himself be dead within the year. Two months passed and his solemn prophecy was fulfilled.

Those who treasured the Jeremiah tradition no doubt faced many different situations which bore some resemblance to the yoke of Babylon. Details are not accessible, since much of the subsequent history of the Jews is lost, but they were always under the thumb of one imperial power or another. Certainly the same issue was alive in Jesus' day, when the Romans were in charge. Elements in society then were optimistic of throwing off their yoke. Remember when Jesus was asked whether it was right to pay taxes to Caesar: his answer gave no encouragement to the revolutionary cause. Indeed his refusal to be the kind of second David that the Jews expected led to the cynically trumped-up charge that this was just what he did purport to be. And while Jesus went the last step which took him to the cross, the road he walked had already been paved by Jeremiah years before.

Some readers of these words may be in a political situation which gives ready-made relevance to such discouragement of zealotry. But most of us need to dig deeper to apply the encounter which Jeremiah had with Hananiah to our own circumstances. But the heart of the matter is a debate between the need to honour obligations however irksome, and the temptation to cut loose from any relationship which does not suit us. In this light it all takes on a very modern profile.

The long book of Jeremiah has a great deal to say about covenants and it is significant that the breaking of the one with Babylon was interpreted as rebellion against God. The message in a nutshell is that though we have obligations to God, it isn't simply that we have not honoured them, but that we cannot of ourselves honour them. Or to put the matter in another way, life throws at us its Nebuchadnezzars which are far beyond our power to manage. This sad conclusion is rubbed in by the repeated warning in Jeremiah that the state of Judah was coming to an end which nothing could avert. But it also contains the passage, well-known from its presence in the Methodist Covenant

Service, which promises a new covenant to take the place of the one which human beings have irrevocably broken.

As far as our relationship with God goes, the promise means that we are offered a new start to remedy a situation in which we can do nothing from our side to put things to rights: this is what the New Testament means when it says that Christ died for our sins, or that the wine at Holy Communion stands for the blood of the new covenant, which Jesus shed on the cross. But we are also offered a new start in the sense that intolerable earthly obligations now become tolerable.

If you throw off the wooden yoke, an iron one takes its place. Christ's yoke may look forbidding and so may the obligations he asks us to honour. But he called it an easy yoke, and this is because it is a double one which he shares with us: his risen presence can enable us to cope with the kind of vice-like pressure which Hananiah mistook for something that could be nonchalantly shrugged off.

Sunday 8th: This day my mind has been calmly stayed on God. In the evening I expected to meet about thirty people in class; but to my great surprise there came near two hundred. I found an aweful, loving sense of the Lord's presence, and much love to the people; but was much affected both in body and mind. I was not sure whether it was right for me to exhort in so public a manner, and yet I saw it impracticable to meet all these people by way of speaking particularly to each individual. I, therefore, gave out a hymn, and prayed, and told them part of what the Lord had done for myself, persuading them to flee from all sin.

Sarah Crosby

The witness of the Wesleys which, under God, brought Methodism into being sprang from a rediscovery of the scriptural way of conscious salvation, as expounded by great teachers and saints of the Christian past. John and Charles Wesley entered into that heritage; their contribution was to explore its spiritual riches, and to guide their own and succeeding generations to that store of spiritual health and wealth.

Henry Carter

Not merely in the words you say,
Not merely in your deeds confessed,
But in the most unconscious way
*   Is Christ expressed.*

Is it a beatific smile?
A holy light upon your brow?
Oh no! I felt his presence when
*   You laughed just now.*

For me, 'twas not the truth you taught,
To you so clear, to me so dim;
But when you came to me you brought
*   A sense of him.*

And from your eyes he beckons me;
And from your heart his love is shed;
Till I lose sight of you – and see
*   The Christ instead.*

Beatrice Cleland

I was in an underground train, a crowded train in which all sorts of people jostled together, sitting and strap-hanging – workers of every description going home at the end of the day. Quite suddenly I saw with my mind, but as vividly as a wonderful picture, Christ in them all. But I saw more than that; not only was Christ in every one of them, living in them, dying in them, rejoicing in them, sorrowing in them – but because he was in them, and because they were here, the whole world was here too, here in this underground train; not only the world as it was at that moment, not only all the people in all the countries of the world, but all those people who had lived in the past, and all those yet to come.

I came out into the street and walked for a long time in the crowds. It was the same here, on every side, in every passer-by, everywhere – Christ . . .

After a few days the 'vision' faded. People looked the same again, there was no longer the same shock of insight for me each time I was face to face with another human being. Christ was hidden again; indeed, through the years to come I would have to seek for him, and usually I would find him in others – and still more in myself – only through a deliberate and blind act of faith. But if the 'vision' had faded, touched by a ray of the Holy Spirit is like being a tree touched by the sun – it puts out leaf and flowers, bearing fruit and blossom from splendour to splendour.

Caryll Houselander

The Fellowship of Christ

Eddie Lacy

The most amazing encounter of my life took place on 24th May 1954. As a young man of seventeen I had recently become involved in a youth fellowship at the local Methodist church. There was nothing particularly spiritual about my presence in the group. I was, indeed, deeply sceptical and even antagonistic towards religion in general, and the organised church in particular. I saw myself at least as a sceptic, if not as a convinced, though very immature, vocal rejector of the Christian way, and yet I was intrigued, and as my discomfort grew I enquired more. It seemed to me that within this Christian fellowship, and especially embodied in the minister and the youth leaders there was some special gift, some attractive luminosity, some hidden strength which, not possessing, I envied.

On 24th May, after some conversation and a brief prayer, I stood to leave the house of our youth leader. He laid his hands upon my shoulder and said, 'All you need is faith.' At that moment, with the most startling clarity and in a moment of total exultation, I knew that the Jesus of whom I had heard others speak, the person who was proclaimed so faithfully in Sunday worship, was there. As real, indeed more real, than the man whose hands rested on me. That encounter quite simply shattered all my previous views and brought me to sincere Christian faith. My spirit rejoiced within me: Jesus was real. I remember cycling home and, at the top of my totally tuneless voice as I rode through the marketplace in York, I sang the only words from the hymnbook I knew:

> Blessèd assurance, Jesus is mine:
> O what a foretaste of glory divine!

A year later when I was beginning to prepare for local preacher's exams I read my first biography of John Wesley. I could hardly believe my eyes when I came across his journal entry for 24th May, for wasn't that the precise day when I too had come to my moment of faith? What was even more astonishing was that the journal entry said that this happened 'at about a quarter before nine'. For the indelible memory of my own conversion moment was also rooted in time and place. Hearing the words 'All you need is faith', my eyes had looked beyond the youth leader to the clock on the mantelpiece where it was precisely 8.45pm, or, in Mr Wesley's phraseology, 'a quarter before nine'.

It was this amazing conjunction of date and time that helped to place my own experience within an historical context. One of the wonders of the evangelical emphases is that there is an urgent stress upon a personal decision. One of the enriching emphases of a wider church perspective is that we belong to a community of faith, and inherit so much from others as we journey on.

The second encounter was also an historic one some time later, when I read the biography of David Hill who was perhaps the first and greatest Methodist missionary to China. The introductory chapter began with a description of my own city, and the first page ended in these words, 'He that is born in York always claims with an affection and pride that need no bluster that he is a citizen of no mean city.' An allusion, of course, not just to York, but to Paul's words in Acts 21:39 when he too claimed to be a citizen of no mean city. What was more startling for me, however, was that David Hill had been brought up in Fossgate almost in the centre of the city; I remembered that was where my own parents' married life had begun, in rooms above the warehouse where the paints and ladders of the family decorating business were stored. If it wasn't the same house then, by its description, it was probably the one next door.

Perhaps this sense of history was born in me earlier on because the grammar school I attended as a boy was just outside the city walls, and in those lessons where I failed to be totally riveted I could look out of the classroom window and see the bar walls opposite the school. I would drift away into a dream-world and imagine Roman legionnaires walking the ramparts of the city and peering out at the forested wilderness where our school now stood. It was only later, of course, that I realised those bar walls were built by the Normans shortly after 1066 and that no Roman soldiers would actually have walked upon those ramparts. Nonetheless, I do have two Roman pennies, one of Septimus Severus, whose headquarters were for a while in York, and the other of Constantine, who was called from York to become Emperor, the first Emperor to embrace the Christian faith.

This sense of the communal as well as the personal, of the historic as well as the present is, for me, encapsulated in the Communion Service. For though our Orders of Service express in a dignified way much of the liturgy of the church, there are times just before we receive Communion when I feel a compulsion to add one of the prayers from the old Order of Service for the Burial of the Dead. It is these words that I find so moving:

> Father of spirits, we have joy at this time in all who have faithfully lived, and in all who have peacefully died. We thank thee for all fair memories and all lively hopes. For the sacred ties that bind us to the unseen world. For the dear and holy dead who compass us as a cloud of witnesses and make the distant heaven a home to our hearts.

Paul, John Wesley, David Hill and Constantine; they are my ancestors, part of the communion of saints, part of the fellowship of Christ that spans time and space, the church militant and triumphant. In some way in encountering Christ I have been drawn into a worldwide and universal communion that is part of my history and my being. It has nothing to do with personal worth or merit. It is entirely the product of divine love and amazing grace.

I met a stranger yestere'en:
I put food in the eating place,
Drink in the drinking place,
Music in the listening place.
And in the sacred name of the Triune,
He blessed myself and my house,
My cattle and my dear ones;
And the lark sang his song,
*   often, often, often*
Comes the Christ in stranger's guise
*   often, often, often*
Comes the Christ in stranger's guise.

Ancient Celtic rune

On my first visit to the abbey, I attended compline in the early hours of a winter evening. In the darkness, with the candlelight dancing shadows in the wide open spaces of the chapel, the deep musical voice of Mother Abbess rang out in blessing: 'May the Almighty and merciful Lord, Father, Son and Holy Spirit bless and keep us.' Later I met the owner of that voice, a small, graceful woman whose dark eyes twinkled with down-to-earth humour. As she described her role, 'I have leadership, but it is to help the sisters on their way to God. I am here to serve. One only leads by experience, and the grace is there if you are humble enough. I have found that my interests have widened immensely. One cares more, and in Christ we can take the needs and sufferings of the world into our hearts.'

International Christian Digest

If this letter reaches you, Bill and I have gone out together. We are very near it now, and I should like you to know how splendid he was at the end – everlastingly cheerful and ready to sacrifice himself for others, never a word of blame to me for leading him into this mess. He is not suffering luckily, at least, only minor discomforts. His eyes have a comfortable blue look of hope, and his mind is peaceful with the satisfaction of his Faith in regarding himself as part of the great scheme of the Almighty. I can do no more to comfort you than to tell you that he died as he lived, a brave, true man – the best of comrades and the staunchest of friends.

Captain Robert Scott

He would resort most commonly to those places and preach in those hamlets lying far away in steep and craggy hills, which other people had dreaded to visit, and which from their poverty as well as upland rudeness teachers shunned to approach. Tarrying in the hilly part, he would call the poor folk of the country to heavenly things with the word of preaching as well as the work of virtuous example.

Bede, speaking of St Cuthbert

Oft have I seen at some cathedral door
A labourer, pausing in the dust and heat,
Lay down his burden, and with reverent feet
Enter, and cross himself, and on the floor
Kneel to repeat his paternoster o'er;
Far off the noises of the world retreat;
The loud vociferations of the street
Become an undistinguishable roar.
So, as I enter here from day to day,
And leave my burden at the minster gate,
Kneeling in prayer, and not ashamed to pray,
The tumult of the time disconsolate
To inarticulate murmurs dies away,
While the eternal ages watch and wait.

Henry Wadsworth Longfellow

As soon as he got up upon the stand, he stroked back his hair and turned his face towards where I stood, and I thought he fixed his eyes on me. His countenance struck such an awful dread upon me before I heard him speak, that it made my heart beat like a pendulum of a clock, and when he did speak, I thought his whole discourse was aimed at me. When he had done, I said, 'This man can tell the secrets of my heart.'

John Nelson, on hearing John Wesley preach

61

Night Flight

Mary Lou Redding

Several years ago I was on a late-night flight out of Philadelphia. There were only a few passengers on the plane, and I was seated in a row alone. As we took off, I looked across the aisle to see the lights of the city as the plane banked to the left. When I did I noticed a young man, perhaps in his late twenties, seated alone one row back, in the window seat. Tears were washing down his cheeks, and he wiped them aside with the back of his hand. I wondered what was distressing him so, and I began to pray for him.

After a while, I decided that praying was not enough. I had to reach out to him in some way, even though we were strangers. I had never done anything like this before, and nervously I got up and crossed the aisle. I sat down and said, 'I don't mean to intrude, and if you want me to go away just say so and I will. But I couldn't help noticing that you are upset, and I wondered if it would help to talk about it.'

He began to talk. He was returning from visiting his mother, who was dying of cancer. He was one of several siblings, all of whom lived closer than he. His father and the other family members were not able to talk with his mother about her impending death. He had always had a special closeness with her, and they had talked openly and at great length about what was happening. He had been holding in all the pain while he was with her, and now he could hold it in no longer. I listened. Occasionally I asked a question but mostly I just listened. He talked about her and about his family. My mother had died not long before this, and I understood that the pain he was feeling was not something I could make go away. So I felt no need to offer advice or solutions. I simply listened. I didn't try to cheer him up or steer the discussion to other things. He talked for most of the flight. We exchanged business cards before I left the plane, and I assumed that the encounter had ended there.

Several months later, at Thanksgiving time, I received a note from him. He wrote of his mother's death, and thanked me for doing 'so much' for him. It had made a real difference, he said. In the years afterward we corresponded from time to time, and always he referred in some way to my 'great kindness'. What was my great deed? I listened. That is all.

That experience taught me a wonderful and freeing lesson. It taught me that we don't have to have answers to help those in pain. In fact, we may help them most effectively when we refrain from offering answers. We simply encourage them to open their hearts. The Bible story of Jesus and the blind man Bartimaeus (found in Mark 10:46-52) has helped me to think about this. In the story, Jesus turns aside to notice Bartimaeus and to listen to him. Calling out to Jesus for mercy, Bartimaeus was apparently something of an embarrassment to his fellow townspeople. One translation of the Bible says that they 'sternly ordered' him to be quiet. But Jesus stopped what he was doing and went to Bartimaeus. He noticed this man in need. And then Jesus asked, 'What do you want me to do for you?'

I find that question remarkable. This was a blind man, so at least one need was obvious. But Jesus did not assume that he knew what Bartimaeus wanted or needed from God. Jesus did not assume what he should be asking God to do for the man. He waited to hear what Bartimaeus would name as the cry of his heart. He did not offer solutions; he invited Bartimaeus into conversation and allowed him to set the limits of their interaction. That is a model we can all follow in our daily encounters.

As we interact with others, we may be tempted to assume that we know what they need and want, especially if we know them well. But no matter what need may seem obvious to us, we cannot know what others seek from God. And we cannot 'fix' them anyway; only God can do that. We do not set priorities for what gets attention. We simply allow those we meet to tell us what is in their heart. We receive them in love, and we listen. That is the example Jesus gives us. And I earnestly believe that when we do so, healing often follows, as it did for Bartimaeus.

In the years since I met that young man on the flight from Philadelphia, I have often forgotten how important it is to create an atmosphere in which others are encouraged to speak. Sometimes I even want people in need to be quiet, as the townspeople urged Bartimaeus. Neediness in ourselves or others can be untidy. It can intrude on all the other, more socially acceptable things we have on our agendas. And when I do acknowledge a need, my first impulse is to act, to do something. But what people hunger for most is someone to notice them, to acknowledge that they matter, that their needs and feelings matter. When I respond to those in distress, they may name some need to which I can respond (and should, in Christian love), but often they ask primarily that I care and take time to let them know I do.

To use Henri Nouwen's phrase, I have learned that we all can be 'wounded healers'. We don't have to be perfect or have the answer to life's dilemmas, and in fact we may be more effective when we realise that. Doing so frees me from the self-delusion that what happens in all the world around me depends on me. It also frees me from the burden of thinking that I must have answers and energy to take care of the entire world. I am not responsible for seeing that all of anyone's needs are met. I am not capable of meeting them, anyway, and God does not intend that I try. But God does call me often to turn aside, to reach out to someone who seems troubled, to listen, and by doing so, to show them that I care and that God does.

We allow God's grace to flow through us when we receive others lovingly. When we do so, we participate in bringing the healing that God wills for each of us.

A Methodist minister of fifty years once described a dream he had had. He thought he was a tourist in heaven and wandered into the museum of that Holy City. 'There was some old armour there, much bruised with battle. Many things were conspicuous by their absence. I saw nothing of Alexander's nor of Napoleon's. There was no Pope's ring, not even the inkpot that Luther is said to have thrown at the devil, nor Wesley's seal and keys, nor the first Minutes of Conference, nor the last . . . I saw a widow's mite and the feather of a little bird. I saw some swaddling clothes, a hammer and three nails, and a few thorns. I saw a bit of a fishing net and the broken oar of a boat. I saw a sponge that had once been dipped in vinegar, and a small piece of silver . . . Whilst I was turning over a common drinking cup which had a very honourable place, I whispered to the attendant, 'Have you not got a towel and basin among your collection?' 'No,' he said, 'not here; you see, they are in constant use.'

Gordon S. Wakefield

An old man was seated alone in the last pew of the village church. What are you waiting for?' he was asked, and he answered, 'I am looking at him and he is looking at me.' People pray not only that God should remember them, but also that they should remember him.

Anonymous

Jesus, we look to thee,
Thy promised presence claim;
Thou in the midst of us shalt be,
Assembled in thy name.

Thy name salvation is,
Which here we come to prove;
Thy name is life and health and peace
And everlasting love.

We meet, the grace to take
Which thou hast freely given;
We meet on earth for thy dear sake,
That we may meet in heaven.

Present we know thou art,
But O thyself reveal!
Now, Lord, let every bounding heart
The mighty comfort feel.

O may thy quickening voice
The death of sin remove;
And bid our inmost souls rejoice
In hope of perfect love.

Charles Wesley

One evening, about fifteen years ago, a little prayer group met in our house. We began, as we always did, by sharing some of our experiences during the week, some of our own needs and perplexities and the needs and pain of those who had asked for our prayers. We talked about the meaning of meeting in Jesus' name and the reality of that presence. Then we went together into prayer . . . This particular evening, a number of unusual things happened. One person was able to share a deep, hidden grief she had not talked about for forty years. Another felt the burden of an angry resentment lifted from her heart. Another experienced release from chronic bodily pain. Another shared with us a clear guiding answer to a perplexity he had prayed about. Another group member felt the closeness of God's love more deeply than ever before.

Flora Slosson Wuellner

The Light of the World is the title of a famous picture by Holman Hunt painted in 1854. It portrays Christ, thorn-crowned, and carrying a lantern, knocking at a closed door. When the artist showed the completed picture to some friends, one pointed out what seemed to be an omission. 'You have put no handle on the door,' he said to Holman Hunt. The artist replied, 'We must open to the Light – the handle is on the inside.'

Anonymous

Three Encounters

Avril Bottoms

> These troubles and distresses that you
> go through in these waters are no sign
> that God has forsaken you; but are sent
> to try you, whether you call to mind
> that which heretofore you have
> received of his goodness, and live upon
> that in your distress.

These words of John Bunyan have been a source of hope and comfort for many years. But I was to take them more to heart four years ago when I had cause to think that I was indeed 'sinking in deep waters; the billows go over my head, all his waves go over me'.

I was in a hospital bed in the private London Clinic, with chronic post-operative trauma and low blood pressure, hovering between consciousness and unconsciousness. Sheer mental and physical frailty had rendered me an absolute wreck, in a wheelchair, weighing six and a half stones, and barely able to stand unaided. I no longer recognised myself when I looked in a mirror. In fact I did not look at myself for almost three months because I found it too distressing.

I was most fortunate to have had brilliant and successful abdominal surgery, after many years of suffering, by one of the foremost consultant surgeons in his field at a specialist London hospital. My convalescence, however, was far from ideal. Instead of progressing I didn't realise that I was in fact slipping back. There were complications which terrified me. The final straw came when I could neither eat nor drink because of sores which developed in my mouth and on my lips. I began to dread which plague would visit me next.

I was admitted to the London Clinic after my local surgery had totally failed to appreciate the seriousness of my plight. I was immediately attached to a drip and sustained for several days while plans for my treatment were made. It was here, however, that I experienced three 'encounters' on one day which will stay with me for ever. Two were with men I had never met before my illness, and the third with a long-standing friend who has had more influence on my Christian life than he will ever know.

These three men confirmed in me that God had heard my prayers of desperation. I have been most fortunate in my life in many respects, but I can also say, with Robert Burns, that there have been 'some drops of joy with draughts of ill between, some gleams of sunshine 'mid renewing storms'. But I have never doubted God and I think that my mother's greatest legacy to me has been her unshakeable Christian faith, despite her own storms. Nothing shook her faith, and nothing shakes mine.

Nevertheless I was in great distress and I found, at times, as others have found before me, that in some instances God's presence can be most confirmed by his absence. I had called out to him as I stood at a window of my room in the clinic looking out in the weak winter sunshine on to the busy Marylebone Road below. I wondered if I would ever again walk along that road; would I ever again clamber aboard a London bus, be part of the rush and tumble of everyday life? I pleaded with God to renew me in body and spirit.

I knew where I wanted to be – but looking at myself and my condition I considered it too wide a bridge to cross to resume a normal life. How would I ever again regain the strength of mind and body necessary to do just that? In deep despair and utter desolation I collapsed back into my bed. I drifted away. Nurses came and went. I heard voices far away. I sank into a twilight zone where I appeared to be wafted along as if I had wings on my feet. It seemed as if I didn't need to breathe. It was so easy and just as if I was floating away, borne along on a tide that was going out. It felt good. I was somehow unaware of my body because everything appeared to be ethereal . . . Suddenly, and unwillingly, I was brought back from wherever I was by frantic nurses at my bedside.

Some little time later my first 'encounter' of that day was when my consultant physician, Sir Anthony Dawson, supremely eminent in his field, came to see me. He knew my background because we had talked earlier. In tears I told him that I had prayed so hard for God to heal me, so that I could once more be part of normal life. 'But he hasn't,' I said. 'How do you know he hasn't?' he asked. 'Because I am still lying here just as I was before I prayed,' I said in tears. 'God not only moves in a mysterious way, he also heals in a mysterious way. He heals in hundreds of different ways, one of which is through doctors and surgeons and nurses,' he said. 'God is going to heal you through me, but I need your co-operation. To put you back on the road again is going to be a long haul, but you are going to make it.'

From that moment on I felt that God was with me in a new way. The next three weeks passed in a haze as I let others care for me. I did not know whether it was day or night. I felt cocooned in a safe little world and I was totally unaware of anything that was happening in the world at large.

Sir Anthony returned again in the afternoon to bring a friend of his, Professor Robert H. Cawley, who he felt would be best to take over my long-term care. This was my second 'encounter'. Professor Cawley was possessed of a wonderful sense of calm and patience in the most trying of circumstances. He was never in a hurry whatever his workload. After some weeks I was transferred to a longer-stay clinic which was to be my home for the next three months, including a most disorientating Christmas. My festive lunch was liquidised.

Professor Cawley rarely missed a day to check on my condition. Because of medication it was difficult to concentrate and words seemed to swim off the page. My first big task was to learn to read the newspapers again. He would talk to me about current events and church news, and was thrilled when one day I ventured out of the clinic for the first time and walked across the zebra crossing to the newsagents to buy a

London evening paper. That was a day marked out. Professor Cawley encouraged, congratulated, suggested and rewarded. In short he is a quite marvellous man. As the days have gone by we have put my life back together again, bit by bit. Sir Anthony, who sadly died last autumn, was right. It was a long road. But I shall always regard these two men as having rescued me and, along with my surgeons and other friends and colleagues, hauled me back to health and normality.

My third 'encounter' on that particular day was in the evening, when a friend of some years, Rev Dr John Stott of All Souls, Langham Place, came to see me. John Stott stands out supremely among many as the one person who has had most effect on my own Christian life for more than twenty-five years. He read to me the passage from 2 Corinthians 12:9: 'My grace is sufficient for thee, for my strength is made perfect in weakness' (KJV). I found that at that point I needed the certainties of the faith, not speculation.

There is much in popular Christian teaching which emphasises easy victory, power, joy in worship, healing and prosperity, but the reality is more about doubt, sickness and failure. The trial by darkness and frailty is God's instrument, and, 'finding no refuge but Christ', I have found, as others before me, that it is through our weakness that we discover his glorious power.

In the summer of 1995 I required emergency kidney surgery but I have learned again through illness about the providence of God. When you are reduced to be as nothing and are thrown back not only on the mercy of God but on those you need to look to for help and support, I found that his provision is abundant. The Christian life is lived in this tension between solace and tribulation, struggle and victory, joy and sorrow, suffering and balm. I have found that the road to life is narrow and winds through dark and desolate places, but that the road points to the light that overcomes the darkness and which can never be put out.

> Fixed on this ground will I remain,
> Though my heart fail and flesh decay;
> This anchor shall my soul sustain,
> When earth's foundations melt away;
> Mercy's full power I then shall prove,
> Loved with an everlasting love.

> J. A. Rothe, tr. John Wesley

To keep God's door
I am not fit.
I would not ask for more
Than this — to stand or sit
Upon the threshold of God's House
Out of the reach of sin;
To open wide his door
To those who come;
To welcome home
His children and his poor;
To wait and watch
The gladness on the face of those
That are within;
Sometimes to catch
A glimpse or trace of those
I love the best, and know
That all I failed to be,
And all I failed to do,
Has not sufficed
To bar them from the Tree
Of Life, the Paradise
Of God, the Face of Christ.

John W. Taylor

Soon after I became a minister, and while I was still a very young man, a great loss fell on a family in my congregation. The husband died a year or two after marriage. I went to see the widow. Her anguish was of that silent, self-restrained sort which it is always most terrible to witness. There were no tears, not a word about the present agony or about the gloom and desolation of the years to come. Her grief was dumb. I was oppressed by it; I could say nothing. The sorrow seemed beyond the reach of comfort, and after sitting for a few minutes I rose in some agitation and went away without saying a word. After I had left the house I felt humiliated and distressed that I had not spoken; I thought perhaps that it would have been better not to have gone at all. I do not feel so now. Sometimes the only consolation we can offer our friends is to let them know that we feel their sorrow is too great for any consolation of ours.

R. W. Dale

The world is so empty if one thinks only of mountains, rivers and cities, but to know someone here and there who thinks and feels with us, and who, though distant, is close to us in spirit, this makes the earth for us an inhabited garden.

J. W. von Goethe

When Stanley went out in 1871 and found Livingstone, he spent months in his company, but Livingstone never spoke to Stanley about spiritual things. Throughout those months, Stanley watched the old man. Livingstone's habits were beyond his comprehension, and so was his patience. He could not understand Livingstone's sympathy for the Africans. For the sake of Christ and his Gospel, the missionary doctor was patient, untiring, eager, spending himself and being spent for his Master. Stanley wrote, 'When I saw that unwearied patience, that unflagging zeal, I became a Christian at his side, though he never spoke to me about it.'

Anonymous

Strengthen all thy faithful servants. Bring them back that wander out of the way. Raise up those that are fallen. Confirm those that stand, and grant them steadily to persevere in faith, love and obedience. Relieve and comfort all those who are in distress . . . Remember all those who have done good unto us. Grant forgiveness and charity to our enemies, and continue goodwill among all our neighbours. Support the sick with faith and patience. Assist those who are leaving this world. Receive the souls which thou hast redeemed; and give us all a glorious and eternal life.

John Wesley

Encounters with Methodism

Richard Ralph

As an opinionated Anglican schoolboy in Sussex studying for his Oxford University entrance examinations in 1969, I was given tuition for my theology papers by a local Methodist minister who was teaching part-time at the school. When we discussed the Church History syllabus I insisted on spending time with my current heroes, John Newman, John Keble and Edward Pusey. And this was agreed to – as long as I studied the early history of Methodism as well!

Because of its unfamiliarity I found the subject of John Wesley and his kin fascinating: there was a powerful appeal in the purity and certainty of their motivation, in their interest in the urban and rural poor, and their devotion to prison visiting (another of my particular interests). Of course I immediately sensed many common currents between Wesley and the founders of the Oxford Movement. The liturgical response and the evangelical packaging may have been different, but there seemed to be agreement at the important level of what really mattered; and remarkable similarity in the wholeheartedness of the sacrificial response that confessional conviction called forth. A general foundation of deep respect for and interest in Methodism was laid.

My next significant encounter with Methodism was as a mature ordinand to the Anglican priesthood, standing with my fellow candidates in Chichester Cathedral on a warm Saturday in June in 1989. We had undergone three years' training, we had been on our ordination retreat, and were now thinking with prayerful concentration about the grace of divine orders which would change our lives for ever. As we stood around the Bishop's throne awaiting the laying on of hands Charles Wesley's great hymn 'O thou who camest from above' was sung. It was at that point that the powerful charge of Methodist hymnody hit me like lightning. It illuminated most perfectly this defining moment of my life and marked me with an abiding sense of the dreadful holiness of the Christian vocation and the impossibility of life without God's spiritual grace. I suppose I was 'strangely warmed'.

Six years of ministerial life in secular employment passed, when I was enjoying a glamorous life in charge of an élite school for performing arts. My work involved a lot of overseas travel. In 1992, on my way back from an Australian audition tour, I was in Fiji for Easter, breaking my long journey home in an airport hotel. On Easter Day I went for a swim and when I returned to my room to get ready for the day I turned on the radio. The Easter Day worship came from one of the local Methodist churches: I had had no idea of the work of the Methodist missionaries in the South Pacific, or of their trials as they reclaimed for Christ those most beautiful parts of God's world. The lovely voices of the Fijian Methodists singing hymns once more impressed me with the range and the reach of the Methodist proclamation of the Christian gospel. And I have since made many good friends in worldwide Methodism.

One of my tasks in Christ Church, St Leonards-on-Sea, the Anglo-Catholic parish in which I have served since 1987, was to lead the recitation of the office of Evening Prayer. This was followed by a meditation – a prayerful interlude which the celebrant could fill as he wished. In my case I conducted the meditation by using devotional words drawn from various sources. There was one such devotion using Newman, another using the Curé d'Ars, and another using Mother Teresa's writings. When I discovered in the little series *Enfolded in Love* a volume devoted to the writings of John Wesley, 'The Gift of Love', I used his words. They proved to be ideal in this context, and I have subsequently used my Wesley meditation several times. Again the range and reach of the Methodist message impressed me – this time in a rather different way. I was fascinated by the ease and snugness with which Wesley's words matched an Anglican service of a very catholic cast. (I have since wondered at the closeness of fraternal relations between Roman Catholics and Methodists as they join hands over the head of the 'established' church.)

My next and most significant encounter with Methodism began in 1995-6 when I decided to accept the offer of the Governors of Westminster College, Oxford, to become its first non-Methodist principal. I remember being impressed by the 'inclusive' nature of the selection process: I lost count of the small groups of staff and students I was invited to meet in a two-day 'getting to know you' sifting process. The selection panel itself had as many non-Methodists as Methodists on it, and the Methodists seemed as relaxed as the others (perhaps more so) about having an Anglican principal. Such trust, of course, invites scrupulous and specific commitment – but it was a childlike act of faith, and as the Methodists opened their arms to me, I opened my heart to them. It is also worth noting that throughout the selection process I had a strange sense of being prayed for, of being warmed and welcomed by a working and worshipping community as I was drawn in towards its heart.

Contact with the Methodist Church and its people has been a most pleasant feature of my time at Westminster so far. The ink was hardly dry on my acceptance letter before fraternal greetings arrived from Mike Leigh, Principal of Southlands College, and himself a Methodist. What constructive professional friendship my senior staff and I have received from him and his colleagues! I soon identified the Methodist heartlands of the College, centreing around the chapel and its chaplain, Martin Groves, and the Methodist Studies Centre and its director, Tim Macquiban.

I also identified a point of growth in the Methodist staff, scattered around the academic and administrative functions of College – and what a source of comfort and strength they have invariably been to me. Nevertheless, I must admit that it has taken me some time to familiarise myself with their style which is shared by everyone in College, irrespective of their religious backgrounds. Much is expected of me, nothing is ever said, by way of praise or blame: rather, one must pick up hints by what is not said, and by what is done. It is a strangely undemonstrative style, quite difficult to steer by at first, but richly rewarding once its inner promptings and springs are understood. For beneath the subtle hints there is a life of prayerful commitment and shared enterprise – a sense of an intricately inter-connected community united by a common professional purpose and way of doing things.

It is an approach which is respectful of differences and weaknesses, willing always to recognise the weight and importance of the individual contribution to the whole, however unimportant that contribution might appear on strictly objective grounds. This is because the totality of individuals, the community, is the important thing – a model not without its dangers in today's competitive world, but certainly with its attractions for one used to working among the disadvantaged and vulnerable.

The chapel is fully ecumenical and has a variety of services. Before I started I recall a Methodist governor telling me of the High Church Anglican 'goings-on', from time to time, thinking no doubt that they would make me feel at home. But it is not this aspect of chapel life which makes me feel at home – much as I applaud the varieties of religious experience and expression which are reflected in chapel worship. Rather, it is the plainness and simplicity of Methodist worship that has been a revelation to me – particularly the annual Covenant service which is held early in the academic year. It is deeply moving, as well as helpful, to make my declaration beside students and colleagues.

I am profoundly grateful for what the Methodist tradition has given to me over the past eighteen months. It has been a spiritually fruitful encounter. It is a tradition, I feel, that should be proudly defended by its practitioners as a distinctive and vital strand in the witness of the Christian churches: a strand which continues to serve a distinctive and valid revelation of Christian truth. The Methodists have more to celebrate – and share – in their tradition than they often allow themselves to acknowledge. Irrespective of the ecumenical company it keeps Methodism owes it to itself and to the profession of Christ in the modern world, to cherish its important historical roots and to articulate its distinctive, often awkward, contemporary message.

One final encounter. My last interview for the post of principal of Westminster College took place in Methodist Church House in London; and now I meet other Church College principals there twice each term, thanks to the hospitality of David Deeks. On one occasion, as we were coming down the staircase after a day-long meeting, a Roman Catholic colleague (running an Anglican college) turned to me and said what a pleasure it was coming into the building: 'The atmosphere is so calm and everyone is so very welcoming and friendly – it makes you want to become a Methodist.'

All through the Bible we find ourselves in the company of people who, peering into the heart of reality, became aware of the world of the Spirit pressing in upon the world of sense which surrounds us. It is this sense of the 'numinous', the beyond in the midst, the eternal caught in the web of time, the mystery that envelops our mortality, which is the essence of spirituality. The creation of this awareness is the work of the Holy Spirit. It is his breath that moves the mists of our ignorance enabling us to glimpse truths that otherwise would remain hidden. All the way from Adam in the garden to Paul on the road to Damascus the Bible shows us people responding in a thousand different ways to the pressures from the unseen world.

Kenneth G. Greet

Go on, then, in God's name, in the path to which your Saviour has directed you, and that track wherein your father has gone before you. Walk as prudently as you can, though not fearfully. Preserve an equal temper of mind, under whatever treatment you meet from a not very just or well-natured world. Bear no more sail than is necessary, but steer steady . . . He by whom actions and intentions are weighed will both accept, esteem and reward you. And my heart and prayers are with you.

Samuel Wesley, to John and Charles

CHALLENGE

What does the Lord your God require of you?
To walk in all his ways, to love him,
to serve the Lord your God with all your heart.

Deuteronomy 10:12

Encounters of . . . Challenge and Change

Elizabeth Dunn-Wilson

It is strange how, over time, words seem to change their meaning in subtle ways. I have always thought of encounters as implying chance meetings which may or may not become significant. Unexpected people are met in unexpected places, leading to consequences which may have far-reaching results. However, looking at the derivation of the word, it is clear that originally 'encounter' implied a hostile confrontation. One 'encountered' an enemy, someone or something to be opposed. Both Old French and Latin suggest that an encounter is the kind of meeting where one 'comes against' something which needs to be overcome, a threat which must be resisted.

As I have thought about encounters in the context of my Christian experience I have realised that the concept of an unexpected meeting which has radically changed my life, has often been bound up with quite genuine battles. On reflection, I can even understand my own conversion experience in these terms.

I grew up in a Christian family where participation in the life of the church was an accepted fact. It was a few months before my fifteenth birthday when I was invited to lead a session of our Wesley Guild meeting. It was a Sunday evening, and as the meeting would end too late for me to catch a bus back to the village where we lived, I had arranged to spend the night at the home of a school friend. I enjoyed the challenge of the evening's events and the two of us talked for a long time until Anne eventually dozed off. But sleep evaded me.

I remember getting out of bed and looking out of the window which overlooked the flat roof of the garage. When I turned back, everything around me had completely changed. The walls, the furniture in the room, all seemed to have disappeared. I found myself part of a huge crowd of people all pushing and struggling along a road. It was very dark and there was a sense of foreboding hovering over us. People were stumbling and falling to the ground because of the pressure of the crowd. Then I heard a very loud, clear voice speaking to me:

> Turn round and go the other way, and
> take them with you.

I reached down and tried to help a few of the people to their feet and as we turned in the opposite direction, pushing our way against the oncoming crowd, I saw the sky beginning to lighten as though dawn was breaking. Against it, the dark silhouette of a cross stood out clearly.

Then, in a moment, it had all gone and I was just standing in my friend's bedroom. I felt completely overwhelmed by the experience. I knew that I had met God and that nothing in my life could ever be the same again. This unexpected encounter, which resulted in my conversion, had indeed taken place on a kind of battleground. The enemy to be overcome was the dark power of sin. God had called me to follow the way of the cross and had shown me that it would mean a struggle, but it was a journey towards the light and one in which I would be challenged to take others with me.

Later that year I went 'on note' as a local preacher. And so the pattern of my life was set on a course which centred around teaching and preaching. A few years later I married David, a Methodist minister. The years went by marked by the birth of our three children and changes of circuit and school appointments. We were very happy and felt that we were where God wanted us to be.

By the early 1980s I had been a head teacher for a number of years. I had always thoroughly enjoyed my work but now, for some reason, I began to feel a growing certainty that God wanted me to do something different. I felt very strongly that I was being called to the presbyteral ministry of the Methodist Church. I was convinced that this was the right course to take. Then, one day when I was walking along the seafront at Eastbourne I experienced another of those encounters which was to mark a great change in the direction of my life. Someone behind me said:

> You should be working on the other
> side of the sea, not here.

I turned round at once, but there was no one there. Yet the words had been so clear. There was no mistaking what I had heard. God was telling me to offer for service overseas.

Our encounters with God may come as a real shock and completely disrupt the plans we have made for ourselves. At times the battle between God's will and our own may even be quite painful. Not since I was a very small child in Sunday school, when we put on concerts to raise money for missionary work, had I ever thought of working overseas. And now here was this challenge! To accept it would mean that I could not candidate for the ministry. I should really have been in a turmoil of confusion, yet somehow all the restlessness about what direction I should take was gone. God knew where he wanted me to be. I had to learn to be patient. It was not until three years later that David received his own call to overseas service and we were invited to serve with the Methodist Church in the Caribbean and the Americas.

Among our many experiences while we worked in the Republic of Panama were two encounters which I shall never forget, both of which meant taking up a battle against hostile circumstances and situations. When I first met Negra she was leaning on a broom taking a brief rest from her job as a road-sweeper in the busy streets of Panama City near our home in Rio Abajo. She invited me to visit her so, a few days later, I and one of my friends from the church found ourselves sitting on upturned boxes in Negra's dilapidated shack. Its walls were patched with cardboard and rags, and the blue sky was visible through the many holes in the tin roof. It was one of hundreds of similar huts in that shanty town. I held Negra's youngest child in my arms, a tiny scrap of humanity covered with sores and obviously severely malnourished. Her six other children stared at us, listless and weak from hunger, their stomachs swollen with worms. Yet these were some of the more fortunate children, because Negra did at least earn a few dollars from her road-sweeping job.

This was my first confrontation with such poverty and desperate need and it aroused not only my sympathy but also my anger. Why was such misery and deprivation being unchallenged? Maybe it was because poverty, the fearsome opponent in this encounter, had always seemed to be too over-whelmingly powerful. That evening, as I prayed for Negra and her family, my thoughts were drawn to the story of the Feeding of the Five Thousand. Reading it again in Matthew's Gospel the words 'You yourselves give them something to eat' stood out as a challenge which could not be ignored.

We began in a very small way, taking some basic foodstuff to about twenty families with very young children. Gradually, after a great deal of prayer and shameless begging, we were able to set up a small feeding programme at our church. Within a few weeks it was properly organised and several hundred families were being helped. The idea spread and was taken up by other churches in the area. It became an ecumenical project. However, our concern must be not only to meet emergency situations but to encourage the setting up of schemes by which people can learn to help themselves. The project in Panama extended to the provision of seed and tools, and to a venture where church and people co-operated to build a new housing estate which was called 'El Sol Naciente' – 'The Rising Sun', a name symbolic of their new hope.

A few years after this encounter, my husband and I moved from Panama City to the remote Valiente Peninsula in the north-west of Panama. The only way to reach our new home was to make a three-hour journey in a dug-out canoe across the often treacherous waters of the Caribbean. We had gone to set up a Bible school to train evangelists, catechists and church leaders from the many Guaymi Indian villages in the peninsula.

This was a daunting challenge but our previous experience encouraged us. It soon became obvious, however, that only men were coming for training, although in our congregations there were many more female members than there were male. We soon realised that all the church officers, lay preachers and leaders were men. How could we encourage the churches to allow women to attend the training seminars? It was then that I met Señora Murillo, in another of those encounters which was to provoke action against a status quo which seemed to be opposed to Christian belief and practice.

Señora Murillo had refused to be left alone in their remote village when her husband came for a one-week training seminar. On the opening day she helped us in the kitchen, preparing the food and so on, but on the second day she did not come to assist. We found that she had gone to the building where the seminar was being held and was sitting on the ground outside the door, listening intently to everything that was going on. The next day she took a chair which she placed by the door and there she sat again throughout every session. Nobody told her to go away and so on the following day she took her chair inside the classroom. For the rest of the week this quiet, solemn woman took her place in every class, and at the end of the last session she calmly stood up and asked, 'And do I get a certificate like everyone else?' David assured her that, as she had completed the course, she would receive her certificate.

By standing up for her rights as a woman to receive Christian education and leadership training Señora Murillo had taken a step which was to bring about a profound change in attitude within the indigenous church in that area. Other women said they too wanted to receive training. The truth of the Gospel – that in Christ all distinctions, including that of gender, were rendered obsolete – began to take concrete form as the circuit leaders themselves came with the request that we should organise training seminars for the women.

Progress was fast. The women were thirsty for knowledge and for opportunities to serve. When the time came for us to leave, the church was ready to welcome a woman as superintendent of their circuit. A little later, plans were being made for a woman to be trained as one of their lay pastors. She is the daughter of Señora Murillo, whose courage and determination had started the 'revolution'.

My encounter with Señora Murillo led me to a continued involvement in the struggle for increased recognition that women's rights are human rights, and the rights of the girl-child must be a priority in our battle for a world society free of oppression and injustice. On my return to England I became involved in the Women's Network of the Methodist Church. For a number of years we have been actively involved in the campaign against the sexual exploitation of children, which was part of the agenda of the United Nations Fourth World Conference of Women and the Women's Forum held in Beijing in 1995. In Beijing I had encounters with thousands of women from all over the world who had met to promote change which could bring about justice and equality for people everywhere. It was an unforgettable experience, and the knowledge that so many are striving after the same goals and courageously confronting similar obstacles is a great encouragement.

I am writing this in Kenya. From the window of my office I can see the forest which is part of the campus of a new university. I am here to learn and to teach, and yes, I have certainly not lacked challenging encounters since I came here. Let me tell you about one encounter I had very soon after our arrival in this country. We were taken straight from the airport to Limuru where the Methodist Conference was meeting, and there we were overjoyed to meet again many of the friends we had made on previous visits to Kenya. We were drinking tea after the evening meal when one of those friends presented me with a challenge which took me right back to our years in Eastbourne: 'We really do feel that you should consider whether God is calling you to candidate for the ordained ministry.'

Somehow I was not even surprised. I had never lost my sense of God's call, and I had simply tried to respond positively to the varied opportunities he had given to me over the years. Yes, I was much older than when I had first heard the call to the presbyteral ministry, but since then God had taught me so much. I have learned that God encounters us in many ways. Sometimes he speaks directly and sometimes through other people or through challenging situations. I have learned that it has to be God who chooses the time and the way and the place where he is to be served. So now, fifteen years after I had first hoped to candidate, I thank God that I am a probationer minister in the Methodist Church in Kenya.

The confrontational nature of God has given me a vivid sense of being part of the prophetic ministry through which he calls us to face up to situations which need to be changed both in our own lives and in church and society. These 'encounters' do contain an element of threat but they also offer a wonderful opportunity for fulfilment. There is one more thing of which I am convinced. In all these challenges we can have absolute confidence that God will guide and strengthen us.

The Lord said,
'Say, "We." '
But I shook my head,
Hid my hands tight behind my back, and said,
Stubbornly,
'I.'

The Lord said,
'Say, "We." '
But I looked upon them, grimy and all awry.
Myself in all those twisted shapes? Ah, no!
Distastefully, I turned my head away,
Persisting,
'They.'

The Lord said,
'Say, "We." '
And I,
At last,
Richer by a hoard of years
And tears,
Looked in their eyes and formed the heavy word
That bent my neck and lowed my head:
Like a shamed schoolboy then I mumbled low,
'We, Lord.'

Karle Wilson Baker

Plunge a stone into a pond and the water moves in rings and ripples out to the bank; plunge a life in the ocean of the love of God, and countless other lives will be affected; plunge, corporately and communally, year after year, generation after generation, and who can count the blessings, wave after wave, that will beat on the shores of this tired world?

Source unknown

It was to me a great discovery when I passed from the thought of doing work and asking God to help me to do it, to the faith that God is doing work, and the prayer that he would let me help him to do it.

Father Andrew

Thou art never weary, O Lord, of doing us good. Let us never be weary of doing thee service. Let us take pleasure in thy service and abound in thy work and in thy love and praise evermore. Fill up all that is wanting, reform whatever is amiss in us, perfect the thing that concerneth us, and let the witness of thy pardoning love ever abide in all our hearts.

John Wesley

If Love should count you worthy, and should deign
   One day to seek your door and be your guest,
   Pause! 'ere you draw the bolt and bid him rest,
If in your old content you would remain.
For not alone he enters: in his train
   Are angels of the mists, the lonely quest,
   Dreams of the unfulfilled and unpossessed,
And sorrow, and Life's immemorial pain.
He wakes desires you never may forget,
   He shows you stars you never saw before,
   He makes you share with him, for evermore,
The burden of the world's divine regret.
How wise you were to open not! – and yet,
   How poor if you should turn him from the door.

S. R. Lysaght

> *Love ever gives —*
> *Forgives — outlives —*
> *And ever stands*
> *With open hands,*
> *And while it lives,*
> *It gives.*
> *For this is love's prerogative —*
> *To give — and give — and give.*
>
>   *Anonymous*

When we are willing to abandon ourselves and to fling ourselves outward in compassion and in service, we find that we have made room not just for others in our lives but also for God in our hearts. The energy that we have massed in our own little centre is spent on others, leaving an open space where God may enter. From this same God-infused centre also flows the renewing energy that allows us to keep loving and serving in the world . . . True obedience, then, is both a listening to what we hear within us and to what we hear beyond us. It is being attentive to those we encounter in our daily lives. It is creating the empty, open space within us where we can hear God speak.

Thomas R. Hawkins

The positive attitude of love, no matter that we slip and make mistakes, is of prime importance. Life is about relationships, and any doctrine which encourages us to build bridges, be sensitive to others' needs, to relate well to people of all backgrounds and origins must be good news . . . Christian perfection may not be attainable in this life except perhaps in a relative sense, but it is the goal to which all Christians look; it can inspire within us a positive attitude of love towards God and neighbour, and remains a main plank of our faith.

W. R. Davies

The Man

Edmund Banyard

This man he made the leper whole
He gave the blind their sight;
The deaf found they could hear again
To darkness he brought light;
And cripples found they had been healed
While silent lips became unsealed.

But we are blind who will not see
And lame who will not walk,
And we are deaf who will not hear
And dumb who will not talk;
Captives, we do not seek release
We do not want his way of peace.

To him the name of God was love,
His kingdom was for all;
The lost he welcomed home again,
The outcast heard his call.
To those who sought the promised day,
He was the life, the truth, the way.

This man destroys our peace of mind
We cannot bear his eyes;
Just let us follow our own paths
Don't point us to the skies.
We want to walk in ancient ways
Content and cosy all our days.

We cannot bear this nonsense of
A God for everyone.
We'll serve the God who cares for us
As we have always done.
We dare not let this man go free
So nail him to the gallows tree.

For the fulfilment of his purpose God needs more than priests, bishops, pastors and missionaries. He needs mechanics and chemists, gardeners and street sweepers, dressmakers and cooks, tradesmen, physicians, philosophers, judges and shorthand typists . . . I do not serve God only in the brief moments during which I am taking part in a religious service, or reading the Bible, or saying my prayers, or talking about him in some book I am writing, or discussing the meaning of life with a patient or a friend. I serve him quite as much when I am giving a patient an injection, or lancing an abscess, or writing a prescription, or giving a piece of good advice. Or again, I serve him quite as much when I am reading the newspaper, travelling, laughing at a joke, or soldering a joint in an electric wire. I serve him by taking an interest in everything, because he is interested in everything, because he has created everything and has put me in his creation so that I may participate in it fully.

Paul Tournier

All loving – but thy love is stern
And claims, not love alone, but deeds:
It profits little if I burn
With rapture, while my brother bleeds;
Further my love with practical intent,
Lest it evaporate in sentiment.

Anonymous

I kneel to pray
and know not what to say;
I cannot tell
what shall be ill or well.
But as I look
into thy face or book,
I see a love
from which I cannot move,
And learn to rest in this.
So would I pray
only to have thy way
in everything, wise Lord
and King.
Grant me but grace
in all to give thee place:
To have thy will perfectly. Amen.

Medieval prayer

When Life says to us, 'Enter on a course of work,' it says, 'Enter, and sometimes fail, and live through the failure.' If it says, 'Work and live with other people,' it says, 'Live with, and care for, those who will sometimes hurt you and sometimes be hurt by you; and bear both.' If it says, 'Go and carry out an ideal,' it includes, 'Go and carry it out, often imperfectly; and make mistakes, and have doubts, and take all the pain of this as well as the pain of right doing.'

Helen Wodehouse

I ask that I may be permitted to love much, to serve to the utmost of my capacity, and to keep faith with that high vision which people call God. I shan't do it wholly. Nobody does that. I only want never to stop caring.

Winifred Holtby

The more you are interested in the incarnation, the more you must be concerned about drains.

Henry Scott Holland

God has made us like members of a body, needing one another's help. For what discipline of humility, or pity, or patience, can there be if there be none to whom those duties are to be done? Whose feet will you wash, whom serve; how can you be least of all, if you are alone?

St Basil

Notice outside a North London church: 'Wanted: Workers for God. Plenty of overtime.'

Anonymous

O God,
Whose disturbing presence
will not leave us be
but breaks through
the forms and patterns
that we fashion for our own protection;
may your Spirit so liberate our hearts
that we abandon the security
of familiar ways
and surrender ourselves in trust
to your unpredictable purposes,
through him who gave himself
entirely to your will,
even Jesus Christ our Lord.

Anonymous

Patience in God's sight depends on the conformity of your will to his. This transforms the torrent of your nature with its floods and shallows into a steady navigable river. It changes you from an agitated, blundering help, plunging impetuously into a useless task yet absent when the Master requires you, into a steady and trustworthy servant on whom he can rely.

Phillipe Vernier

Encountering a God with Passion!

Fran Beckett

As the turbulent final years of the twentieth century draw to a close, and we face a new millennium stretching out before us, what signs of hope for the future are there?

Life in our Western post-modern age is characterised by a preoccupation with 'me first', with what we hold to be important shaped and influenced by personal experience rather than objective truth. Notions of community and neighbourhood have been considerably eroded, and the predicted continuing upward trend in the number of single person households in the UK indicates a growing insularity from one another in society.

Discussions about and portrayals of various expressions of love fill our TV screens, and pack the pages of tabloid newspapers and popular magazines. Love means different things to different people. Tragically, for far too many it is associated with regret or pain. Experiences of loss, being let down or even abused and exploited in the name of love can be listed in the catalogue of human misery over this subject. And as perhaps both a symptom and a cause of this, lifetime commitment in relationships is now regarded as something of an oddity, still largely desirable but maybe, nonetheless, a somewhat idealistic or naïve expectation.

Yet, within us all, there is a hunger for tenderness and for a sense of belonging with someone else. The amazing outpouring of public grief at the death of Diana, Princess of Wales in 1997 was, at the time, attributed by many to a widespread desire for a more caring society. The continuing popularity of TV soap operas like *EastEnders* or American cult programmes like *Friends* point us towards a society that is preoccupied with human relationships, desperately wanting them but not always knowing how to handle them.

What has all this to do with God? What relevance has he to our problems in trying to relate to each other?

In the pages of the Bible we encounter a God who cares about this world and the people in it. He loves the unlovely and unlovable. He cares that people are oppressed by sin and all its effects. His is not a slushy, saccharine-sweet, naïve sentimentalism but a tangible, passionate and active love that knows the worst we can do and loves us just the same. That love is the lifeblood that he wants to put in our veins, not just for us but for the good of a needy, hurting world.

This God cannot be ignored. We encounter him in the white hot intensity of his anger against oppression and exploitation, expressed by the prophets who populate the pages of the Old Testament. This is no weak, insipid God but one who burns with a zeal for justice, love and holiness. He is not lukewarm or half-hearted in responding to this world. Again and again, he demonstrates a particular concern for those who are poor or vulnerable, urging his people to defend their cause. This side of God's character is sometimes easier to forget. It is something that can make us feel uncomfortable, so we keep it at the margins of our minds. The radical nature of his zeal can too easily impinge upon our lives, causing disruption and forcing a troubling re-examination of our priorities.

God is passionate about people, and not just as isolated individuals. Community is at the heart of the Godhead, somehow contained in the mystery of the Trinity. Themes of community and principles for human relationships can be found in Old and New Testaments alike. Mistakes and failures are not glossed over but faced up to squarely, with God himself repeatedly giving those who let him down the opportunity to be fully restored in relationship with him. Here we see commitment to relationship radically modelled by God himself rather than just being an ideal to which we are somehow to aspire.

In God's passion for people, we encounter something more than theory, doctrine or mere head knowledge. We are drawn into the very heart of the living God. Here we see a tenderness and compassion that is breathtaking in its scope, yet a solidness and reality that means that God's passion is more than feelings alone. We see this supremely in Jesus. It was as if God rolled up his sleeves, meaning business in order to sort out the mess his once beautiful creation had got into. In Jesus, he stepped into human history, into the midst of the pain and sin that grips the world. He identified with us, sharing our humanity with its joys, frailties and pressures.

The challenge of the incarnation is that God didn't love us from afar. His love motivated him to come among us, to get involved not as an untouchable angelic being but as flesh and blood, living in relationship with people like you and me. He embodied his message time and again as he fed the poor, gave special attention to those socially excluded by others, healed the sick, and knelt to wash his disciples' feet, so showing them the lengths to which his love would go.

This God, full of passion for people, whom we encounter in the pages of the Bible and in the person of Jesus is the hope that we can have as we enter a new millennium. In our success-geared society, where people are valued by their level of income, academic qualifications or actions alone, rather than for just being people with an inherent dignity and worth, he has much to teach us. It is about a commitment to one another that is based on valuing the other person for themselves and a willingness not always to pursue our own rights or aspirations. Loving someone is about stickability, being there for them, not always necessarily agreeing with them, but nonetheless offering a safe place where they can be themselves. It is about getting involved with people, identifying with others as God identified with us in the incarnation.

However, encountering our passionate God faces us with an even bigger challenge. He calls the church to live out his passion in the world around, modelling his love and justice not just in our relationships together as

Christians but also through our commitment to those in need. He calls us to share his priorities in embracing a hurting world, treating the most unlovely of people with dignity and affirmation. He challenges us to step outside the comfortable safety of what is familiar to us. He calls us to risk sharing in his zeal for love and justice to be worked out in society, investing into building a sense of community amongst people who are very alone.

When faced with all of this, it is understandable that we might be tempted to retreat into just pursuing our personal lives. Maybe it is all a bit daunting, or our individual sphere of influence seems too limited. However, it is worth remembering that one snowflake on its own melts on the cheek but a snowstorm can stop the traffic! In other words, together with each other and God we can make a difference. The challenge and the wonder of encountering a God with passion is that we can never truly be the same again . . .

I saw you in the morning, Lord,
As the sun rose in the sky;
But I had to get to work,
So I simply passed you by.
I didn't want to see those eyes
Looking, pleading with me, or
That outstretched hand from the pavement,
With its shadow of Calvary.

I sensed you in the noontide, Lord,
Reading the papers of the day;
But other people's problems
Could not get in my way.
For I knew that time was short,
And I wanted it all for me,
So I closed out what it was I felt,
With its memory of Calvary.

I heard you in the evening, Lord,
When it came to the nine o'clock news;
But I was tired so I switched the side
To something inclined to amuse.
I didn't want to hear those cries –
They couldn't be meant for me –
So I listened to something easier
Than the echoes of Calvary.

I looked for you at my sleeping, Lord,
When I came to my resting place;
But I could not find you anywhere,
For I had not known your face.
I'd never sensed or heard you, Lord,
None of that was for me;
For I was too busy, and time was too short
To live with Calvary.

Lorna Lackenby

O Lord God and Father, you know how blind we are to your presence, how dead to your purpose and deaf to your call; grant us to feel your guiding hand through all the scattered details of our daily life, in all the tumult to hear your still small voice, and in all dimness of our spirits to have a sense of your everlasting arms upbearing us, so that, being willing to spend and be spent in your service, we may accomplish all that you would, and at the last find fulfilment in the perfect freedom of your sole sovereignty.

Source unknown

In the saving of the world God seeks to join men and women with himself and his Christ, and calls them to work and labour with him until evening.

Anonymous

We shall hear [God] not only in the still depths of our being and in our time of prayer and worship, but also in the unexpected places. We shall hear him in the people we meet, in the stories people share; we shall find him in the problems we confront and in the freedom we seek on others' behalf.

Ann Bird

Pour thy grace into my heart, O Lord, that I may worthily magnify thy great and glorious name. Thou hast made me and sent me into the world to do thy work. Assist me to fulfil the end of my creation by giving myself up to thy service. Prosper whatever I shall undertake this day, that it may tend to thy glory, the good of my neighbour, and the salvation of my own soul.

John Wesley

Beloved,
You have all the gifts you need;
I know, because I gave them to you;
You have skill and insight,
experience and care.
You have faith and love to move mountains –
as small as a mustard seed, I mean, but
that is enough.
So, go, and be my ambassador.

Denis Vernon

You must do as well as ever you can whatever God gives you to do; that is the best possible preparation for what he may want you to do next.

Thomas Chalmers

> *Lord of the loving heart,*
> *May mine be loving too;*
> *Lord of the gentle hands,*
> *May mine be gentle too;*
> *Lord of the willing feet,*
> *May mine be willing too;*
> *So may I grow more like to thee*
> *In all I say or do.*
>
> *All Our Days*

God did not tell us to follow him because he needed our help but because he knew that serving him would make us whole. Our work for God – our service – adds nothing to his power or his achievements. He does not need anything we can give him, not even our obedience. But that does not mean that our work and service for him is meaningless or without value. God has promised to those who serve and follow him life, immortality and eternal glory. These rewards are specifically for servants who actually serve, and followers who actually follow.

Irenaeus, 4th century

Stepping Stones or Stumbling Blocks?

Roger Royle

Born a cradle Christian, the church has always been part of my life. It dominated my first year as I was a child of the vicarage and, even though my father died when I was one, it continued to call the tune. My mother was a very committed churchgoing Christian. Her involvement was one hundred per cent. Girl Guides, Mothers' Union and the flower rota, alongside very regular weekday and Sunday worship set the pattern for her free time, while during the working day she was absorbed as a dedicated teacher in a church school.

In a letter to the secretary of the Parochial Church Council, thanking them for their support after the sudden death of my father, she vowed to bring her children up in the way that my father would have wanted. And so, not being someone to break her promises, my brother and I were brought up as children of the church. We were both servers and choirboys at home, and the boarding school to which we were sent was a church foundation, which took religion seriously.

During my early years it was through the church that I encountered God. But over the years that has changed. The sudden death of my mother, when I was still at school, brought about a change in my life. Despite the total commitment of my mother, the organised church let me down. Admittedly we didn't live in the parish, but in order to get the vicar to visit us to make arrangements for her funeral, we had to send a car for him.   And after the funeral, in the week before I returned to school, I can't remember a single visit or 'phone call from anyone involved in the day-to-day running of the church as an organisation.

What I did experience was the love, care and real concern of individuals. Many of them were committed Christians but quite a few were not. And although I never regretted my ordination, I have learnt over the years to look to individuals, rather than to the organisation of the church, if I wanted 'to see Jesus'.

As an organisation I have needed the church. It has provided a focus and a structure in my life. But over the years I have come to realise that instead of the stepping stone on your journey to God, as it is meant to be, it can become a very real stumbling block. Position can become more important than people. Buildings take preference over belief. Status is emphasised more than service. It doesn't surprise me that many people, who call themselves Christians, sit lightly to their commitment to an organised church. With some it will be idleness but for many the medium gets in the way of the message. It is the structure that they see and not the spirit within it.

Increasingly I have encountered God through individuals, through people who are not only made in the image of God but reflect that image in a most powerful and influential way.   Blind people have helped me to see. Badly disabled people have helped me to move freely. The bereaved, the lonely and people who would be regarded as insignificant have given me a purpose in life. And from ordinary, run-of-the-mill people I have been shown what loyalty and commitment really mean. A church organisation is often so concerned about its structures that it forgets the people it is called to serve. So instead of reflecting God, it becomes yet another human organisation with all its petty squabbles and confused sense of priorities.

Obviously this isn't true of all church communities. Those that are real communities reflect both the power and the love of God. It often has nothing to do with size, but has everything to do with commitment, just as God's relationship with us is based on commitment:

> God so loved the world that he gave his only Son, so that everyone who believes in him may not perish but may have eternal life. God did not send the Son into the world to condemn the world, but in order that the world might be saved through him.
>
> John 3:16-17

It was because of God's love for the world that he sent his Son. He was not selective in his love, nor was he half-hearted about it. The sending of the Son showed total commitment. The love for the world showed unearned, indiscriminate love. Jesus didn't come for the chosen few. He came so that everyone should have the chance to respond to him. He didn't come to condemn. He came to save, to give new life. Compare that with what we often do as a church. We can be very selective in our love and we can be judgemental in our attitude. We become a stumbling block over which people fall or which they avoid totally so as not to get involved.

Throughout his life Jesus constantly challenged the stumbling blocks that organised religion had set up. Lepers were touched. Samaritans were acknowledged. The mentally sick were accepted. Petty human rules were broken. The insignificant were made significant. The love of sinners was accepted. It cost him his life but it set a standard for us to achieve. It is interesting that it was to Peter, a disciple who had really let him down, that Jesus gave the command 'Feed my sheep.'

Failure was never ignored by Jesus. Nor was it condemned. It was faced and hopefully transformed. He became the stepping stone through and over which people could travel to a more realistic life where they could be at peace with themselves and in love with others. My concern is that organised churches are trying to put the clock back. Structures and status have become all-important. As the number of regular churchgoers diminishes, so the attention the church pays to itself seems to increase. It is no wonder that the world, the world that God so loved, passes by on the other side. The time that the Church of England has taken and is taking discussing the ordination of women, the ordering of services and the ordination of homosexuals knows no limits. And yet the outside world has come to terms with many of these issues without the help or guidance of the church. Women are seen as having an equal part to play in society as men. Communication, be it sacred or secular, has got to make sense, and homosexuals are recognised more for their gifts rather than their challenge to the so-called norms of society. The world has come where people are. The church organisation has passed by on the other side.

Where it *has* come where people are, its witness has been wonderful. Take the Hospice movement. The great taboo of the world has been tackled head-on by Christians. Hospices are the best current example of witness to the Risen Christ that I know. People feel that they matter, and not just those who are physically sick but their relatives as well. The spirit and the soul are cared for as much as the body and the brain. Life after death is seen as a joyful reality to be accepted rather than as a total emptiness to be feared. Here in the hospice are real stepping stones.

It was Fiona, a young, severely disabled woman who taught me more about righteous anger than anyone else I know. She also taught me how to transform anger. We had had supper together and then had watched *Coronation Street*. She then wanted to show me something she had written on her computer. She indicated that it reflected her feelings. Her disability had been particularly cruel, and she also had to face other emotional difficulties in her short life, so I would not have been surprised to see on the screen a whole string of swear words or abuse. Instead the text was the first eight verses of Psalm 55. The psalmist is at odds with God. He is distraught and he is not afraid to say so. He longs for the wings of a dove, so that he can escape and leave all his problems behind. Life had become too much for him, as it had for Fiona.

However, had Fiona written out the full psalm she would have seen that the tone changes. The psalmist calls to God and he is saved. He recommends others to 'cast your cares on the Lord and he will sustain you'. The anger is overcome and a purpose for life is found. As I read that passage with Fiona it was my job to stop it becoming a stumbling block and transform it into a stepping stone. And not just for her, but for myself and for those who loved her.

Stumbling blocks on our pilgrimage through life can be turned into stepping stones, but only if we tackle them. The division between the churches is a real stumbling block which prevents many from experiencing a true encounter with God. It will be only when divisions are broken down, status and structures are put in their rightful place and all people are allowed to see Jesus that those stumbling blocks will be removed and the church organisation will become once again what it is meant to be, a stepping stone.

Forth in thy name, O Lord, I go,
My daily labour to pursue,
Thee, only thee, resolved to know
In all I think, or speak, or do.

The task thy wisdom hath assigned
O let me cheerfully fulfil,
In all my works thy presence find,
And prove thy acceptable will.

Thee may I set at my right hand,
Whose eyes my inmost substance see,
And labour on at thy command,
And offer all my works to thee.

Give me to bear thy easy yoke,
And every moment watch and pray,
And still to things eternal look,
And hasten to thy glorious day.

For thee delightfully employ
Whate'er thy bounteous grace hath given,
And run my course with even joy,
And closely walk with thee to heaven.

Charles Wesley

Prayer is great but in the last analysis human need is greater. Florence Allshorn, the great missionary teacher, used to run a training college for missionaries. She knew human nature and she had little time for people who suddenly discovered that their quiet hour was due just when the dishes were to be washed! Pray we must; but prayer must never be an escape from reality. Prayer cannot preserve a man from the insistent cry of human need. It must prepare him for it; and sometimes he will need to rise from his knees too soon and get to work – even when he does not want to.

William Barclay

It is unlikely that we will hear God's voice calling us to risk, to move out in new mission or with new vision, if we are very comfortable and settled with things the way they are. And most important of all is a great love of God and a passion for his will. When these elements of faith in God, desire for his way (dissatisfaction with our way), and great love for him and his will are present in a solitary life or a community, the possibility of one hearing God's voice of guidance is greatly multiplied.

Reuben P. Job

God wants a person; he cannot send a thing, nor a machine, nor a sound. God wants us not to aid him in guiding the stars in their courses. For us, God's business is with human lives, human souls. What God has in view is the salvation of the lives he has created, of the souls which he has made.

C. J. Vaughan

Really to pray is to stand to attention in the presence of the King and to be prepared to take orders from him.

Donald Coggan

The self is only itself, healthy and whole, when it is in relationship, and that relationship is always dual, with God and with other human beings.

Eugene H. Patterson

Those who bring sunshine to the lives of others cannot keep it from themselves.

J. M. Barrie

Let love and appreciation have their way. So many tired hearts might go on their way singing at the mere price of a handclasp, a whisper of encouragement, or a look which told that some loving service has not passed unnoticed. In our concern for the peoples of the world let us also give a thought to the starving hearts in our own household.

Great Thoughts

We act in a world in which Christ has already acted, and we seek to align ourselves with him in the belief that his way – the way of love – is the way things ultimately are and that in him our work will not be in vain.

David Anderson

If I could give you information of my life, it would be to show how a woman of very ordinary ability has been led by God in strange and unaccustomed paths to do in his service what he has done in her. And if I could tell you all, you would see how God has done all, and I nothing. I have worked hard, very hard – that is all – and I have never refused God anything.

Florence Nightingale

Till the End of Time

Arnold Kellett

A very special kind of encounter, reserved for the privileged few, is to be interviewed on *Desert Island Discs*. There, in the guise of an intimate one-to-one conversation, you reveal your thoughts to millions. The nearest I have come to this experience was last year when I was invited to be a guest on Radio York's equivalent of this programme – an hour's chat and record-choice called *Talking to Elly*.

The questions were all very sensible, and I had a lovely self-indulgent time talking about my past life and choosing my favourite music. I started with one of my boyhood records – still a great favourite – Suppé's rousing overture *Poet and Peasant*. My penultimate choice was from Bach's *Mass in B Minor*, which I had heard performed magnificently in York Minster. Then, for my last record, I went from the sublime to pop, and chose a song which had just been released by the new group, Olive:

> You're not alone –
> I'll wait till the end of time for you . . .

I chose this partly because it seemed ideal for a lonely castaway and partly because the words and melody had been written by our son Tim, formerly with Simply Red, but now with a group of his own. By coincidence the very day of the broadcast his song was announced as Number One, and Olive was overwhelmed with radio and TV appearances.

Though my kind of music is the classics, I genuinely like this song, not only for the way it is sung, but also for the words. They take a well-worn path, of course, and remind me of Robert Burns in his wonderful 'Red, Red Rose' poem, speaking of how he will love his girl 'till a' the seas gang dry/and the rocks melt wi' the sun'.

Yet to love someone until 'the end of time' is clearly impossible. We appreciate the poetic licence of Burns and others who use this image to express their passion and devotion, but time extends beyond the lives of individual lovers. You can love someone until your own ration of time expires, but long after you are dead there will still be time.

If, however, the singer means that he or she will love the other person 'for ever', then we must bring in the concept of moving from time into eternity. 'Love is as strong as death,' says the Song of Solomon, and we have many other scriptural hints that love, allied to faith, transcends the destructive finality of death. The supreme Christian hope is not only that we live on in the new dimension of reality we call eternity, but that, as the 'resurrection of the body' implies, we live on as individual personalities, reunited with those we love.

But what about 'the end of time'? What an intriguing phrase this is! What do we mean by it? It is as difficult to conceive of the end of time as it is the beginning of time. The biblical doctrine of Creation has been remarkably supported in recent years by the almost general acceptance of the Big Bang theory. Did this event occur within time, or did the beginning of time coincide with the beginning of everything? Similarly, when everything comes to an end – when, as Emily Brontë expressed it, 'suns and universes cease to be' – will time then come to an end, or will it continue for ever?

Such philosophical speculations may get us nowhere, but they make us aware of the limited nature of our tiny mortal minds, and we turn with relief to the concept of Almighty God, the incomprehensible ground of all being, who has graciously revealed himself to us in Jesus, the Eternal Word who became flesh and blood, living amongst us and dying for us. Moreover we have the promise of the Risen Lord that he is with us 'till the end of time' (Matthew 28:20).

As the millennium approaches there is more and more talk of the end of the age, when the present world-order will be wound up and superseded. Both fairy-tale cults and extreme Christian groups are telling us that 'the end is nigh'. And so it is, but not in the way they think. Leaving aside the doctrine of the Second Coming of Christ – and there can be no doubt that this is part of orthodox Christian teaching – the world will vanish and time will come to an end for every one of us . . . at the point we call death. I know that individual death is not the same as global or universal death, but from a practical point of view it amounts to the same thing. When we die, to all intents and purposes, that is the end of time as we know it.

We should never allow ourselves to be deceived by the illusory nature of time – a point tellingly made by Charles Wesley in his wonderful New Year hymn:

> Our life is a dream,
> Our time as a stream
> Glides swiftly away,
> And the fugitive moment refuses to stay.

And it was plain ordinary dying that he surely had in mind, just as much as the Second Coming, when he went on:

> The arrow is flown,
> The moment is gone;
> The millennial year
> Rushes on to our view, and eternity's here.
>
> HP 354

None of this I find depressing. On the contrary, it is stimulating. The realisation that time is limited, rapidly running out, is a spur to greater endeavour. I recently made a pilgrimage to Dr Johnson's birthplace in Lichfield, and I thought of his complaint about John Wesley. He was a good conversationalist, he admitted, but instead of sitting back and folding his legs for a leisurely chat Wesley was forever looking at his watch, 'always obliged to go at a certain hour'.

Modern Methodists, too, should keep an eye on their watches and clocks. The end of time, the midnight hour, presses upon us. There is so much to do, so little time left in which to do it. It really is always later than we think. True, there is a place for recuperative leisure and prayerful meditation. But these are the springboards from which we plunge into renewed activity. 'We must work while there is still daylight,' said Jesus, 'It will soon be night' (John 9:4).

There is a sense in which our encounter with God will not occur until we are transferred from time into eternity. In popular speech when people die we may say they have gone to 'meet their Maker', and Charles Wesley's hymns are full of the idea that the glimpses we have on earth are only a foretaste of the real thing in heaven. Yet there is a sense in which we meet God in every fleeting moment of ordinary life. It is as though he is there, personally dispensing our precious allocation of time. Nor will he ever disclose to us just how much time we have left, which only emphasises how carefully we must use our 'residue of days or hours' – to the glory of God and in the service of our fellow men and women.

Written above the clock on the ancient tower of our parish church here in Knaresborough is a phrase of St Paul's – 'Redeeming the Time'. In modern English this means something like 'Make the very most of the time you have left. Use the present opportunity to the full.' God meets us in the moments, each one coming to us as a challenge. He is the Lord of time as well as of eternity.

Salvation, as every Methodist should know, is not by works, through what we do. But when we stand before the Judgement Seat of Christ in heaven, we shall be made acutely aware of how we have used our time on earth.

GODHEAD

Give ear, O heavens, and I will speak;
for I will proclaim the name of the Lord;
ascribe greatness to our God!

Deuteronomy 32:1&3

Face to Face with the Messiah

Michele Guinness

[Michele Guinness was brought up to observe all the traditions of her Jewish culture. But an encounter with a Christian friend made her question her beliefs, and she turned to the Bible to try to find the answers.]

Although my mother had expressly forbidden New Testament lessons at school, I sometimes lingered at my desk longer than I should, taking an age to gather my books and leave the classroom. Or I stood with one ear to the closed assembly hall doors. I wanted to hear more about Jesus. He did not seem to have done any wrong that Jews should treat him so disparagingly. In fact all I had managed to piece together was the picture of one of the most extraordinary beings who had ever lived. Christians revered and worshipped him. Could they all be misguided? When it came to numbers they had more right on their side than we did. Mother said proudly that that was because we Jews did not proselytise like the Christians. We did not want converts, but I was never convinced that that was the answer.

That night, as I read about him for the first time, Jesus Christ lived for me. This was no remote historical character of two thousand years ago, but someone who was vibrantly alive now, in the present. He became as real to me as the people I sat next to on the bus every day, with the difference that none of them was like this man. He was utterly unique, totally compelling. Every gesture, every word mattered, not just because they made sense out of the mess our world seemed to be, but because they spoke directly to me. That was what was so extraordinary. The more fascinated I became the more I felt our relationship was reciprocal.

'Don't be a fool!' I told myself. 'A man who died all those years ago! How can he read your thoughts?' Yet everything he said confirmed the growing feeling that he knew me with a startling intimacy. Nothing seemed hidden from him, no question, frustration or longing, none of the nasty pieces of selfishness that went on in my little head. It was an uncomfortable feeling but I neither wanted to run away nor defend myself with a protective covering of self-righteousness. What was the point? For Jesus, mankind was obviously an open book. Besides, instinct told me that he would not reject me, but rather, unbelievably, that he loved me and had been waiting for me to give him my attention all along . . .

I read on until one particular statement which Jesus made halted me with a start:

> In my Father's house are many rooms;
> if it were not so, would I have told you
> that I go to prepare a place for you?
>
> John 14:2

I read it over and over again to make sure I had read it properly. I could hardly believe that here was the answer to the one question which had haunted me for years. No one, not even the rabbis, had ever spoken to me confidently about heaven before. 'Do your best,' they said, 'and then one day, perhaps, who knows . . . ' A 'maybe' was not good enough for me. If there was nothing beyond the grave, then death made a mockery of every day we lived. Why do your best for something that might not exist? Why live at all?

Was it possible that Christ was right, that there was such a thing as life after death, that he had room in heaven for me too one day? No, it was too good to be true, a fairy story. Who was I to say that generations of Jews had been wrong? What did I know about theology? Still, I could reason it all out as well as anybody else. If there was no heaven or hell, Christ was a liar. How could a man who spoke so much that rang true for me be a liar? He might have been deluded, suffered hallucinations. Then he would have been locked up somewhere for safety . . . But he seemed to suggest he was God. No other Jewish prophet had ever done that before. That was blasphemy. What was left? Only that he was who he said he was, the Messiah, the one my people had been awaiting for so many years.

I shut the Bible, thrust it under my pillow, switched off the torch and tried to get some sleep. My mind was racing. 'Take up your cross and follow me.' What did it mean? If I followed Christ, would I have to say goodbye to my family, friends and traditions, the only life I had ever known? They would certainly say goodbye to me. Oh no, God, no, not that, I can't.

Get a grip on yourself, stop being so silly, who are you talking to anyway? A God who lives way beyond the galaxy in untouchable splendour. As if he cares about a tiny dot like you!

The next night I got my Bible out and began to read again. Philip, the disciple, seemed to put my dilemma into words:

> Lord, show us the Father, and we shall
> be satisfied.
>
> John 14:8

That was it, what did God look like? I had never dared formulate a mental picture of God before. There are never any paintings of him in Jewish books or synagogues. That would be a transgression of the commandment never to make a graven image. Somehow that had transferred itself to painting pictures in my imagination too. Christ's reply took me aback:

> Have I been with you so long, and yet
> you do not know me, Philip? He who
> has seen me has seen the Father.
>
> John 14:9

I understood. The very things which attracted me to Christ reflected the personality of God, his Father. At last I could give my imagination the freedom it longed for. I could begin to see God.

* * * * *

Some six months [later] a school trip to York was arranged to see the Mystery Plays . . . I had not realised that the Mystery Plays were medieval interpretations of biblical stories from creation to the end of time, but somehow seeing the Bible portrayed like that as a whole made me realise just how much of the New Testament was a continuation and completion of the Old.

As darkness fell the lights on the immense stage beneath us were turned up, and the performance took on a magical quality. The crowds around me ceased to exist. The hard wooden bench which moments earlier had seemed to bite into my backside no longer vied for my attention. I was entranced, aware only that as we moved inexorably on to the crucifixion we were reaching the climax of the evening. Christ was on trial, was booed, hissed and rejected. A vast cross was dragged across the stage and the Roman soldiers stripped him and nailed him down with blows that resounded across the York Castle grounds. As the cross was hoisted into the air with Christ stretched out upon it, suddenly everything fell into place for me, and I understood what I had been reading for the last few weeks. I wanted to leap up and down and shout, 'That's it! I've got it! That's why Christ had to die, so that I can be forgiven and have eternal life,' but I held on tight to the bench instead.

I was dizzy with excitement. All the self-reproach, the sense of failure and emptiness which had weighed me down for years and made me feel unable to look God in the face was offloaded onto that cross and hung there with Christ. This was the real freedom he spoke about. Blow the cost. I would follow him whatever it meant.

The performance ended. People got up, laughed and chattered. I sat very still. I did not want to move. I wanted to hold on to every minute for as long as possible, to try and make some sense of it all. Someone dug me playfully in the ribs with the end of an umbrella. In a daze I followed the other girls back to the guest house, almost unable to speak for the strange gurgling sensation in the pit of my stomach. I wondered whether to stop one of them, but what would I say? 'Something very important happened to me tonight.' It sounded a bit forced, even a bit corny, so I said nothing and sauntered along in my own little world, blithely oblivious of everything around me. Besides, I had neither the comprehension nor the vocabulary to explain whatever it was that had happened to me that evening, although I knew I should never be the same again.

> *Bewildered, lost, I must stand still;*
> *Alas, I can no further go.*
> *Wilt thou not, Lord, thyself reveal?*
> *I want, I wait thyself to know.*
>
> *This moment, if thou ready art*
> *To make in me thy humble home,*
> *Break even now upon my heart;*
> *My Saviour and salvation, come.*
>
> *Charles Wesley*

In the stillness of the evening, O Father God, I would still my mind and heart, to become aware of your all-pervading Presence; I would cast out of me all the warring emotions, all the disharmony, all the poisons which disturb the mind. And I would become increasingly conscious of the reality of your peace round me and in me. I would close my eyes to all outward things and know the only Truth, yourself, dwelling within me, giving me harmony, unity and the strength of thy peace.

William Portsmouth

God wants us to come to him and be happy, but he does not make the mistake of trying to force us into happiness. He is not like the mother on the sands who had one of her family in a fractious mood. As she finished thrashing him, she was heard to say, 'Now will you be happy like the others?'

Garfield Wade

It is hard to find words in the language of men to explain the deep things of God. Indeed, there are none that will adequately express what the children of God experience. But perhaps one might say the testimony of the Spirit is an inward impression on the soul, whereby the Spirit of God directly witnesses to my spirit, that I am a child of God; that Jesus Christ hath loved me and given himself for me; and that all my sins are blotted out, and I, even I, am reconciled to God.

John Wesley

O God, some of us are not sure concerning thee; not sure what thou art; not sure that thou art at all. Yet could we ever think these things unless thou thyself wert very near?

W. E. Orchard

Love bade me welcome; yet my soul drew back
    Guilty of dust and sin.
But quick-eyed Love observing me grow slack
    From my first entrance in,
Drew nearer to me, sweetly questioning
    If I lacked anything.

'A guest,' I answered, 'worthy to be here.'
    Love said, 'You shall be he.'
'I, the unkind, ungrateful? Ah, my dear,
    I cannot look on thee.'
Love took my hand and smiling did reply,
    'Who made the eyes but I?'

'Truth, Lord, but I have marr'd them: let my shame
    Go where it doth deserve.'
'And know you not,' says Love, 'Who bore the
        blame?'
    'My dear, then I will serve.'
'You must sit down,' says Love, 'and taste my
        meat.'
    So I did sit and eat.

George Herbert

If we only have eyes to see, each day we shall find great surprises. For ever God is placing for us, in unsuspected corners, gifts which tell of his love. It is true that he answers the prayer, 'Give us this day our daily bread.' The bread he gives us is for body, mind and soul.

W. Bardsley Brash

When we have come into a personal relationship with God . . . there is an underlying sense of satisfaction or peace. This comes because we are aware, however dimly it may appear at first, that it is through our contact with God that we shall ultimately find the answer to our deepest needs, and the richest fulfilment of our personal life. It is true that we do not find all questions immediately answered, for example, in the problem of pain or of evil, yet because God is a personal presence, there often comes a satisfying answer at an even deeper level, giving us confidence and trust even in the face of intellectual uncertainty.

John Baker

The Stranger

Mike Hollow

Who is this chippy,
this hippy,
this lippy young man from the sticks?

Who is this creature,
this preacher,
this teacher who's so full of tricks?

Who is this wheeler,
this dealer,
this healer who raises the dead?

Who is this stranger,
this danger,
this manger-born breaker of bread?

Who is this leader,
this feeder,
this pleader for justice and grace?

Who is this singer,
this covenant bringer,
this flinger of stars into space?

Who is this sower,
this grower,
this knower of all that I am?

Who is this mender,
this sender,
this tender redeemer, the Lamb?

Who is this maker,
this shaker,
this breaker of death's final sting?

Who is this pastor,
this forty-day faster,
this Pharisee blaster,
this demon outcaster –

My Master,
my God
and my King.

I am no longer anxious about anything; for he, I know, is able to carry out his will, and his will is mine. It makes no matter where he places me, or how. That is rather for him to consider than for me; for in the easiest positions he must give me his grace, and in the most difficult his grace is sufficient. If God places me in great perplexity, must he not give me much guidance; in positions of great difficulty, much grace; in circumstances of great pressure and trial, much strength? No fear that his resources will be unequal to the emergency! And his resources are mine, for he is mine.

James Hudson Taylor

Enter this door
As if the floor
Within were gold,
And every wall
Of jewels, all
Of wealth untold;
As if a choir
In robes of fire
Were singing here,
Nor shout, nor rush,
But hush!
For God is here.

Inscription in St George's
Church, Boscombe

Imagine a family of mice who lived all their lives in a large piano, just as we live our lives in our fragment of the universe. And to them in their piano-world, came the music of the instrument, filling all the dark spaces with sound and harmony. At first the mice were very much impressed by it. They drew comfort and wonder from the thought that there was someone who made the music – though invisible to them – above, yet close to them. And they loved to think of the Great Player they could not see. Then one day a daring mouse climbed up part of the piano and returned very thoughtful. He had found out how the music was made. Wires were the secret; tightly stretched wires of graduated lengths which trembled and vibrated. They must revise all their old beliefs: none but the most conservative could any longer believe in the Unseen Player. Later, another explorer carried the explanation further. Hammers were now the secret, numbers of hammers dancing and leaping on the wires. This was a more complicated theory, but it all went to show that they lived in a purely mechanical and mathematical world. The Unseen Player came to be thought of as a myth.

But the pianist continued to play the piano.

The Observer

All our life is a festival; being persuaded that God is everywhere present on all sides, we praise God as we till the ground, we sing hymns as we sail the sea, we feel God's inspiration in all that we do.

Clement of Alexandria

His presence is not bound
To vast cathedrals and the light that falls
Through many-tinted glass. His voice and
*   touch are found*
Within the poorest doors, the humblest walls.

He sits at table with the tired and poor,
He shares the fireplace with the spent and old,
He keeps with suffering a vigil sure,
And plays with childhood in the summer's gold.

His feet refuse no threshold, want and care
Do not repulse him, no, nor even sin.
Wherever need is waiting, he is there,
Where love invites, he enters in.

Anonymous

As I go along I do not whistle to keep my courage up; I sing because I live with God and am beginning to understand how glorious it all is.

James Ellis

The closer we live to God, the more frequent the conversation with him, the greater our understanding of his will and purposes for us.

P. F. Holland

At times in the silence of the night and in rare, lonely moments, I experience a sort of communion of myself with Something Great that is not myself.

H. G. Wells

Grant to us, O Lord, the inward happiness and the serenity which comes from living close to thee. Daily renew in us the sense of joy and let the eternal spirit of the Father dwell in our souls and bodies, filling every corner of our hearts with light and grace, so that we may be diffusers of life, and meet all ills and accidents with gallant and high-hearted happiness, giving thee thanks always for all things.

Lucy H. M. Soulsby

Encountering God

Mark Wakelin

In this piece I will not write of encounters with God on hillsides where the sun shone so deeply in the sky that my soul seemed to turn somersaults, nor the moment of the birth of my children, when all the labours and successes of life seemed for an instant to be wonderfully trivialised and fulfilled at the same time, nor even of moments in worship or prayer when my heart 'was full of Christ and longed its glorious matter to declare'. Instead I want to recount a life-long excitement with ideas and thoughts that have grabbed my mind so that my heart was sent racing, and I became absorbed in the pleasure of a new way of understanding. My encounter with God is through the world of academic theology.

I have been deeply privileged to know Christians who have allowed me to question and think, who have encouraged reflection and honoured doubts; such people were my parents and such, in the main, were my teachers. At a Methodist school I recall religious knowledge lessons with enormous pleasure; the chaplain, Kenneth Wilson, teaching thirteen year olds of the kingdom of heaven in Mark's Gospel; his successor, John Barrett, introducing us to the theology of Rudolf Bultmann when we were fifteen years old and keen; and Laurie Campbell, the headmaster, expecting us to argue, debate and disagree, and respecting us the more for the enthusiasm of youthful wrath and passion.

I still feel the keen happiness I felt when I read the New Testament with a group of school friends in the light of a cursory glance at an introduction to theology. All of us were studying sciences for A level, but we marched fearlessly into the alien world of Bible study with nothing to guide us save an adolescent confidence in our ability to argue. The God we encountered was the iconoclast God – the breaker of idols – not the idols of Baal or Babylon, but the safe and cosy gods of Sunday school and popular sentiment. All was open to question, ridicule and arrogant dismissal, provoking the anguish of believing less and less of what we had until then taken on trust.

I am often told that people who read theology lose their faith. It is not something I fully understand, for I found faith as clearly as any evangelist could hope, while taking notes in a New Testament lecture. I had tasted something of this world through introductory books at school, and felt something of the intellectual struggle in our school Bible studies, but now I was an undergraduate and could argue with the people who wrote the books. While some lectures left me sleepy and confused, some left me so full to the brim that I could hardly sleep at night.

I was encouraged continually to think new things. Stuart Burgess, another chaplain in my happy experience of the breed, delighted in the sharp question and the new idea. He relished the arguments of students in his care, having an endless patience with our dazzling naiveté and unreflecting pride! It was Dr James Dunn during tutorials in the buttery bar who cautioned my arrogance while challenging my faith, and Professor Heywood Thomas who elegantly laid bare the poverty of my thinking. Jimmy Dunn became a sure guide through the thrilling landscape of theology for me, opening me to the peculiar idea that intellectual rigour was a friend of faith and not its sworn enemy. The iconoclast God had shown another side, and the time for building came; the idols had been broken and the foundations laid for new ways of understanding.

It is hard to express the pure joy of hearing some ideas for the first time. I felt as if I wanted to explode; I was unable to remain silent; I felt I simply must explore and argue the new idea. I may have wanted to fight or embrace it, but that didn't matter, for I simply delighted in new thought. I can still recall the sharp, delicious pain of understanding the thrust of Peter Berger and Thomas Luckmann's argument in the *Social Construction of Reality* or becoming almost dizzy with pleasure when I read Peter Brown's *Augustine of Hippo*, and began to grasp the nature of Augustine's crystal-clear Christian philosophy.

You may gain the impression that I was a good student, reading extensively, writing easily, achieving effortlessly. The reality was far from this. I laboured unevenly and was easily distracted. The more I adored a subject, the poorer my essays! I always seemed to do well in assignments that I considered pot-boilers, while my impassioned essay on the 'Christian Platonism of St Augustine', or my complex discussion of 'The Social

Reality of Religion' received lowly marks and much criticism. I am not an academic as I understand and admire the species. This is partly, I suspect, that I am simply too involved, too taken up and changed by ideas. Much that I had to read frankly bored me, and I was far too undisciplined to do more than the minimum when such was the case. But that which challenged me, shook me, turned me around and made me walk a different way – that rare book, that unusual lecture – they stay with me with a persistence and a power that would probably surprise my teachers and amaze my examiners.

I spent three unhappy years at college training for the ministry. I am not sure quite why it was so unhappy. I had, perhaps, expected too much. I probably gave far too little. But even here I could say, 'Surely God is in this place and I did not know it!' It wasn't in the tedium of overly precious lectures on the liturgical dress of the early church, nor in the endless self-indulgence of community meetings, but in the passion of a Pentecostal preacher in my placement in a black majority church in Aston, and in my failed attempt to do postgraduate research at Birmingham University. In the former I heard the excitement of truth that came without the reassuring trappings of academic style, and in the latter I was forced to read German theology 'as if for the first time'.

Here I met a new face of God. The iconoclast God who had begun to build began to challenge me and say, 'Now you must follow!' Fans of German theology will know how fundamentally different it is from Anglo-American theology, so much so that half the battle in understanding it is to let go of all you thought you knew. Whereas home-grown theology begins with the assumption: 'We know what God is like' and asks the question 'Is this God in Christ?', the theology of Dietrich Bonhoeffer, of Wolfhart Pannenberg or of Jürgen Moltmann begins with the assumption: 'We know nothing of God' and asks the question 'What do we learn of God from Christ?' I failed to get my Masters degree, to my long-term sorrow, but I met a different face of God that profoundly affected my future work as a Methodist minister.

To some, theology seems irrelevant, mind games for the Christian equivalent of anorak-wearing train spotters. How can the bleak, dogmatic theology of Karl Barth with all its endless footnotes and depressing analysis contribute to the practical Christian's daily struggle? Well, again, my experience seems to differ from that of the majority. For example, seven years as a hospice chaplain challenged my limited pastoral gifts, and would have found them wholly wanting but for the God I encountered in Moltmann's *Crucified God*. This God – dynamic, moving, suffering, changing, calling me onwards and outwards – this God, brought alive from the pages of the New Testament by an ex-German POW, was the only God who made sense to me of the suffering and anger of my experience. My ministry is filled with countless more examples enough for me to know that, for me at least, the encounter with God through reflection and study is as potent as the God encountered in any other way. Meeting God changes all.

I end with a confession. I read theology only occasionally now. I do still study, however, and continue my research into adult education at the Institute of Education in London. Here I find new challenges in the world of social science, and apply what I learn to the complex question of theological education and ministerial formation. I have achieved more academic success in this field and overcome, to some extent, my profound disappointment in my failures at ministerial training college. But still, unbidden and unlooked for, the God who fills the minds of scholars and flows through their writings catches me out and leaves me breathless. Hidden in an article, running through a well-wrought sermon, influencing an idea, underpinning a book, I encounter the God who through my mind calls out to all of me.

Of course, none of this questions the God found in creation, experienced in fellowship, encountered in worship, discovered as the 'treasure hidden within'. All these I rejoice in, for 'I know that my redeemer lives'. But for the scholars who think deeply and dare to ask questions that I cannot, I thank God. For the God who is secure enough to let me doubt and reason, and needs no-one to guard the truth, I worship and adore. For the truth that is tough enough to take what beatings it has to, and gentle enough to calm the frustrations of the searcher, for the truth that will 'find you out and set you free', I offer all that I am and will be.

> Could we with ink the ocean fill,
> And were the skies of parchment made;
> Were every stalk on earth a quill,
> And every man a scribe by trade;
> To write the love of God above
> Would drain the oceans dry;
> Nor could the scroll contain the whole,
> Though stretched from sky to sky.
>
> Anonymous

While I was reading prayers at Snowsfields, I found such light and strength as I never remember to have had before. I saw every thought, as well as action or word, just as it was rising in my heart; and whether it was right before God, or tainted with pride or selfishness. I never knew before . . . what it was 'to be still before God'.

I waked, by the grace of God, in the same spirit; and about eight, being with two or three that believed in Jesus, I felt such an awe and tender sense of the presence of God as greatly confirmed me therein; so that God was before me all day long. I sought and found him in every place; and could truly say, when I lay down at night, 'Now I have *lived* a day.'

John Wesley

The first thing that you are to do when you are upon your knees is to shut your eyes. Then with a short silence let your soul place itself in the presence of God. That is, you are to use this or some other better method to separate yourself from all common thoughts, and make your heart as sensible as you can of the divine presence.

William Law

Words read, or spoken by friends, a song, a mountain, a sunset or the sea may be God's messengers. In our own thoughts God may use a memory of the past, a sudden new idea, a plan or hope for the future, and can make us realise that he is speaking through it. We can sometimes see how these thoughts come, sometimes it is a mystery: sometimes a thought which we believe holds a message from God comes with force and urgency, sometimes in a slow and tranquil manner. In our times of quiet he uses these inner ways of reaching us, and as we follow him we learn to distinguish with growing assurance his presence in our thinking and our praying, and to 'hear him inly speak'.

Dorothy H. Farrar

You ask, what is this kingdom? And I answer gladly. It is the kingdom of the forgiven heart. It is the still gladness that comes to you through knowing that God is your Father and you his child, and that whatever comes the Father will never hurt and never harm his own child.

Alistair MacLean

Thou shalt know him when he comes
Not by any din of drums,
Nor his gown,
Nor his crown,
Nor by anything he wears.
He shall only well known be
By the holy harmony
That his coming makes in thee.

Anonymous

This Divine Lord desires only that he may rest in thy soul, and may form therein a rich throne of peace, that within thine own heart thou mayest find silence in tumult, solitude in company, light in darkness, forgetfulness in injuries, vigour in despondency, courage in alarms, resistance in temptations, peace in war, and quiet in tribulation.

Molinos

Still, for thy loving-kindness, Lord,
I in thy temple wait:
I look to find thee in thy word,
Or at thy table meet.

Here, in thine own appointed ways,
I wait to learn thy will:
Silent I stand before thy face,
And hear thee say – Be still!

Be still! and know that I am God;
'Tis all I live to know;
To feel the virtue of thy blood,
And spread its praise below.

Charles Wesley

The mystical experience can be thought of as an unusually vivid feeling of the intimate presence of God, which may be accompanied by a profoundly moving and unexpected insight. It is a high-intensity experience, such as may be associated with religious conversion, rather than a low-intensity experience, such as the more placid calm and assurance of ordinary public worship. It is adequately described not by comparatives but only by superlatives. It is a feeling of certainty that one is directly in touch with profound depths of reality which are usually hidden.

Harvey Seifert

Life from God's Point of View

Fiona Castle

My 'encounters with God' generally come from reading his Word and, as I do, the Holy Spirit, the 'still small voice' convicts me of an area of my life which needs changing. Unfortunately, over the years it has happened all too frequently as God continues to challenge and encourage me to change areas and attitudes in my life that are wrong.

This was never more true than at a time soon after I had become a Christian. I went to a Bible study afternoon at a friend's house. A pastor from the local Baptist church had been invited to speak. (I at that time was worshipping at an Anglican church.) He started to read Ephesians 5:21-24:

> Honour Christ by submitting to each other. You wives must submit to your husbands' leadership in the same way you submit to the Lord. For a husband is in charge of his wife in the same way Christ is in charge of his body the church. (He gave his very life to take care of it and be its Saviour!) So you wives must willingly obey your husbands in everything, just as the church obeys Christ.
>
> The Living Bible

(Paul also goes on to give advice to husbands and children and employers and employees!)

The pastor went on to explain it, making it relevant to today . . . isn't it always? He was saying that husbands should be head of their households as 'High Priests' of their families, and that their wives should be submissive to them.

Well! I had never heard such radical teaching. I had quite happily worn the pants in the family, taking responsibility for decisions for their lives, their future, and keeping them under control. How could my husband do that when he was away so much of the time? When the time came for questions at the end of the study I had a fair old argument with the pastor about it which continued after the meeting had finished. He very quietly suggested that I went home and reread the verses and asked God to speak to me through them.

I did, and God began to speak. He showed me that being submissive was not to become a doormat, to have no opinions and no rights. He showed me that because women are the 'weaker vessels' under their husbands' authority they are protected. The husband takes responsibility for the decisions he makes for himself and the family and because of that the wife knows security. As God revealed the truth of this I began to know a deep sense of peace, as I let go of another area of my 'will' and placed it in God's hands. As I began to work it out in practice I marvelled at the wisdom of his 'manual' as it gradually brought a new harmony into the home.

I had to admit that I had usurped my husband's place in the family, denigrating him and preventing him from being all that God wanted him to be in his home. The change was slow and subtle and I'm not sure if my husband was consciously aware of what was happening!

I began to discover life from God's point of view rather than from my own chaotic point of view. I realised I did not have to conform to society's demands and standards. God was calling me to work out his standards, which, although higher, brought a sense of peace which I had never known before.

A Christian friend once gave me this advice: 'I can be as right as right can be, but if I'm right with the wrong attitude, I'm wrong.' So much of life depends not on what we do, but the attitude with which we do it. Does our attitude bring discord or harmony? As I began to learn this new way of living I realised how precious a peaceful, happy home was and how important it was to make sure our home was a haven for the family and a place they would always want to bring their friends.

'Try to live in peace even if you must run after it to catch it and hold it' (1 Peter 3:11). I can only say that this was to stand us in good stead for the rest of our marriage. I thanked God that he shows us the best way . . . not always the most comfortable . . . not the easy options . . . but he opens a door and says, 'This is the way; walk ye in it'; and when we do . . . PEACE!

> *Bless all who worship thee*
> *From the rising of the sun*
> *Unto the going down of the same.*
> *Of thy goodness, give us;*
> *With thy love, inspire us;*
> *By thy Spirit, guide us;*
> *By thy power, protect us;*
> *In thy mercy, receive us;*
> *Now and always.*
>
> *5th century collect*

I left my office at lunch-time, stopped at a small Greek café in Fleet Street to buy some rolls and fruit, and walked up Chancery Lane. It was an August day, quite warm but cloudy, with the sun glaringly, painfully bright behind the clouds. I had a strong sense that something was about to happen. I sat on a seat in the garden of Lincoln's Inn waiting for whatever it was to occur. The sun behind the clouds grew brighter and brighter, the clouds assumed a shape which fascinated me, and between one moment and the next, although no word had been uttered, I felt myself spoken to. I was aware of being regarded in love, of being wholly accepted, forgiven, all at once. The joy of it was the greatest I had ever known in my life. I felt I had been born for this moment and had marked time till it occurred.

Monica Furlong

Eternal God, you are a song amid silence,
a voice out of quietness,
a light out of darkness,
a Presence in the emptiness, a coming out of the void.
You are all of these things and more.
You are mystery that encompasses meaning,
meaning that penetrates mystery.
You are God,
I am man.
I strut and brag.
I put down my fellows
and bluster out assertions of my achievements.
And then something happens:
I wonder who I am
and if I matter.
Night falls,
I am alone in the dark and afraid.
Someone dies,
I feel so powerless.
A child is born,
I am touched by the miracle of new life.
At such moments I pause . . .
to listen for a song amid silence,
a voice out of stillness,
to look for a light out of darkness.
I want to feel a Presence in the emptiness.
I find myself reaching for a hand.

Oftentimes, the feeling passes quickly,
and I am on the run again:
success to achieve,
money to make.
O Lord, you have to catch me on the run
most of the time.
I am too busy to stop,
too important to pause for contemplation.
I hold up too big a section of the sky
to sit down and meditate.
But even on the run,
an occasional flicker of doubt assails me,
And I suspect I may not be as important
to the world
as I think I am.
Jesus said each of us is important to you.
It is as if every hair of our heads were numbered.
How can that be?
But in the hope that it is so,
I would stop running,
stop shouting,
and be myself.

Let me be still now.
Let me be calm.
Let me rest upon the faith that you are God,
and I need not be afraid.

Kenneth G. Phifer

Yield room for some little time to God; and rest for a little time in him. Enter the inner chambers of your mind; shut out all thought except that of God, and such as can help you in seeking him; close your door and seek him.

Anselm

Only at rare intervals does the deeper and vaster world come through into conscious thought or expression, but they are the memorable moments of life. It is then, if ever, that the door to the invisible world silently swings open, and something of the wonder and greatness of the spiritual universe is flashed upon the soul.

A. N. Whitehead

The believer too has known moments on which the calm of eternity seemed already to rest, blessed seasons in which he has beheld not only Moses and Elias, but his own life also transfigured in his beloved Lord; times in which things present were intelligible, things distant clear. And he too has come down to meet the full shock of this world's perplexity. To whom shall he even speak of the things which he has seen and heard? Even while he thinks upon the vision he may find by a sudden blank and stillness in his own spirit that it has been received up again into heaven.

Dora Greenwell

The Final Encounter

Colin Morris

In the eighteenth century, the American Calvinist preacher Jonathan Edwards preached a sermon about the Last Judgement which he called 'Sinners in the Hands of an Angry God'. It is said that women fainted and strong men clung to the pillars of the church to contain their trembling. Whole generations were brought up on such terrifying notions of Judgement which not only inspired powerful preaching but also some of the greatest works of art and poetry.

Now, though the picture-language of the old preaching may no longer speak to our age, the reality of judgement is still central to any understanding of the Gospel. We may encounter Jesus as Master, Saviour and Lord; we will face him as our Judge. This is the final encounter, for as the creed puts it, 'We believe that you will come to be our Judge.' Note, God is not waiting to judge the world but coming to judge it. He does not position himself at the last frontier either of history or of our individual death to encounter us in judgement; he crosses that frontier to meet us as the Word become flesh, for as John's Gospel puts it, 'The Father has handed over all judgement to the Son.' Our judge left footprints in the sand and blood on a cross in first-century Palestine, and he who will confront us in the end is the one who constantly encounters us in our daily lives.

The Gospels are full of encounters embodying judgement. One of the most troubling New Testament incidents is that of the healing of the ten lepers. Jesus heals all ten, but only one, a Samaritan, returns to thank him. The other nine go their way and resume their old life. But why does Jesus accept the situation without protest or complaint? Why doesn't he call the nine back and remonstrate with them, pointing out what a miracle had been done for them and how they were insulting God by their ingratitude? No, he leaves it at that. He accepts their verdict. Presumably, the moral of the story is that God in his own ways and times encounters us, and if we are unmoved by him, the danger is not that in his anger he may consume us, but that he may accept the fact he has failed with us and lets us walk away. God treats us as mature, responsible individuals. We encounter our destiny, we are given our chance, we make our choice, and God accepts it. We have judged him, and in the process we have been judged. That is an appalling prospect.

John's Gospel describes another way in which we encounter Jesus as our Judge. Christ as the Light of the World is an image which makes sense of two of his sayings that apparently contradict each other: 'I came not to judge the world but to save the world', and 'For judgement I came into the world.' Jesus himself reconciles them in another saying: 'This is the judgement, that light has come into the world and men love darkness rather than light.' In other words judgement is the inevitable consequence of any encounter with Jesus. We can get by in the semi-gloom with our deceptions, illusions and half-truths, but when the Day-Star rises and light comes into the world, we are ruthlessly exposed, caught as though in a spotlight doing those things we ought not to have done.

My first church after I left theological college was in the South Yorkshire coalfields and I had a landlady who was fiercely houseproud. Every Monday she washed the bed-sheets and there they flapped in the wind, their sparkling cleanliness not harmed by the fact that they had the pit slag heap as a backdrop. Then one weekend it snowed and the slag heaps were covered in blindingly white snow. Against that backdrop, my landlady's sheets looked just a little less pristine. Judgement by the light.

In the parable of the sheep and the goats, Jesus offered a simple test by which we know when we have stumbled across the one who is our judge. 'Lord, when did we see you . . . hungry, thirsty, naked or a stranger?' Jesus replied, 'Truly I tell you that what you did to the least of these, you did to me.' That's how we know. The question is: did you or did you not answer the cry of distress of your neighbour, whether he or she lives next door or on the other side of the world? We are divinely judged by our answer to that question. Quite simply, what we do to each other we do to God. The voice of almighty God in judgement is not heard booming from beyond the stars but in the cry of the hungry for bread, the downtrodden for dignity, the victim for justice.

Though in the life of the historical Jesus the Last Judgement has already begun, it reaches its climax beyond history. It was Jesus himself who talked of the wrath to come, of sinners being cast into outer darkness, of the worm that dies not and the fire that isn't quenched. He didn't only speak words of consolation and promise but also words of rebuke and grave warning, and when we have made every possible allowance for figurative language and the thought-forms of his time, his meaning is unmistakable. His stern message obviously struck home to the apostolic writers. They declared it as their common faith that 'it is appointed to all men once to die and after that the judgement'.

But how and when and where? With all the limitations history has imposed on us, how can we possibly know what goes on beyond history? In the kingdom of heaven everything is changed; all things are made new because it has to be a resplendent creation able to bear the weight of Divine glory. But the Book of Revelation declares that a bleeding Lamb has been sitting on the throne of the universe from the beginning – it is God in his sacrificial rather than penal aspect whom we finally encounter. I find it impossible to imagine that even in another life there could be a more complete expression of God's love, and therefore of his judgement, than the cross reveals. So the cross is the pinion which locks the old and new creations together; it is the one familiar landmark in a terrain where all else is enwrapped in the strangeness of glory.

Put starkly, if we do not encounter Jesus as Saviour and experience his love as redemption here, we will encounter him hereafter as Judge and experience his love as wrath. But let's be clear that even his wrath is an expression of his love; how could it be otherwise since love is what he is through and through? Just as we must not reduce God's redemptive love to purely human emotion, so we must not think of his wrathful love as being on a par with human impulses of anger. In a lovely phrase, St Augustine wrote that God's wrath does not disturb the tranquillity of his mind. There is no heat, fire, or aggression in it. In a famous incident in the Gospels, 'The Lord turned and looked on Peter, and Peter knew.' No condemnation, no fury, no utter abandonment; just the naked pain felt by love betrayed.

The wrathful love of God is not insensate fury but implacable purpose. God has no more animus against us when we flout his will than a brick wall we crash into is showing its displeasure by flattening us. This is why Paul describes the concept of God's wrath not as a Divine attitude towards us but as the inevitable consequence of cause and effect in a moral universe. The arithmetic must add up in the end. All accounts must be settled because if anything has been overlooked, it cannot be redeemed.

Even God's wrath is a form of love and it is of the nature of love that it cannot bear separation. 'Where art thou?' was the first question God uttered at the dawn of the world as he sought out Adam. I dare to believe that 'Where art thou?' will also be the final anxious question which will ring throughout the new creation as God strives to ensure that none is lost. But that unthinkable fate must be a possibility because God's sovereignty stops short at the point of my free will. I am at liberty to walk away from the Final Encounter. Into what?

There, in that other world, what waits for me?
What shall I find after that other birth?
No stormy, tossing, foaming, smiling sea,
    But a new earth.

No sun to mark the changing of the days,
No slow, soft falling of the alternate night,
No moon, no star, no light upon my ways,
    Only the Light.

No grey cathedral, wide and wondrous fair,
That I may tread where all my fathers trod.
Nay, nay, my soul, no house of God is there,
    But only God.

                    Mary Coleridge

Contributors

Rev Edmund Banyard is a minister and former Moderator of the General Assembly of the United Reformed Church. He is a committed ecumenist and currently edits *All Year Round* for the Council of Churches for Britain and Ireland.

Fran Beckett has been Chief Executive of the Shaftesbury Society for the past two years. She is involved with various Management Committees and Councils of Reference, including the London Bible College, the Evangelical Alliance, Youth for Christ and Pioneer. Fran has a commitment to see churches be 'good news' in the community, and is widely known as a speaker and writer on social action issues.

Avril Bottoms began her career in journalism on the *Derbyshire Times,* and for the past twenty years has been on the London staff of the *Methodist Recorder.* She is deeply rooted in Methodism, at the same time having links with St Paul's Cathedral. Her interests include cathedral music, classical music and concerts, opera, ballet and art.

Rev Jack Burton is a Methodist minister who, after serving in the Glasgow and Ely circuits, was given permission by the Methodist Conference to pursue a 'worker-priest' pattern of ministry. Since 1968 he has been employed as a bus driver by Eastern Counties, and has served as union Branch Chairman and Employee Director. He was elected Sheriff of Norwich in 1988, and has written a number of books, including *England Needs A Revival* (SCM Press, 1995).

Fiona Castle trained in dance and drama, and appeared in shows and pantomimes in the West End. It was here that she was introduced, by a mutual friend Eric Morecambe, to Roy Castle, whom she married in 1963. They had four children. Since Roy's death from lung cancer in 1994, Fiona has worked with the Roy Castle Cause for Hope Foundation, raising funds for the world's first lung cancer research centre. She is the author of *Give us this Day* and *No Flowers . . . Just Lots of Joy* (both Kingsway).

Rev Elizabeth Dunn-Wilson is a lecturer in Christian Education and a Voluntary Ordained Minister in the Methodist Church in Kenya. A teacher by profession, she and her husband served for several years in Panama with the Methodist Church in the Caribbean and the Americas. She has also served as the National President in England of Network.

Michele Guinness is a freelance journalist and broadcaster. She has written several books, including *A Little Kosher Seasoning* and *Promised Land* (both Hodder & Stoughton). She was born into a Jewish family, and is married to an Anglican clergyman.

Celia Haddon is an author and journalist. Her current books are *One Hundred Ways to Serenity* and *If God Is My Father, How Can He Love Me?* both published by Hodder Headline. As the pet agony aunt of the *Daily Telegraph*, she answers readers' queries about their furred or feathered loved ones.

Mike Hollow became a Christian while studying languages at Cambridge. After sixteen years with the BBC he joined Tearfund, where he now works as leader of its editorial team. Mike is married to Margaret and they have two teenaged children, Catherine and David. His poetry has been published in various places, including the wall of Mile End tube station!

Rev John Job was educated at Kingswood School and Merton College, Oxford. After a classics lectureship at Magee University College, his first two posts as a Methodist minister were college and school chaplaincies. Later he was Vice-Principal at the Immanuel College, Ibadan, and returned from Nigeria to be a tutor at Cliff College, where he wrote a book on Job called *Where Is My Father?* (Epworth Press). Before retiring he was Superintendent of the Rugby circuit and during his final appointment in Bedford he was a hospital chaplain.

Dr Arnold Kellett is a Methodist local preacher, and has been a finalist and judge in the Preacher of the Year competition. In 1983 he took early retirement from his post as Head of Modern Languages, King James' School, Knaresborough. He has twice been the town's Mayor. His publications include a dialect version of the Gospels, and *Kellett's Christmas*. He is married with four children and numerous grandchildren.

Rev Eddie Lacy is the Chairman of the Oxford and Leicester District of the Methodist Church. During his time as a minister he has also been a prison chaplain. Recently he has written a series of articles for the *Methodist Recorder*.

Mary Lou Redding is the Managing Editor of *The Upper Room* magazine, an international daily devotional magazine which originates in Nashville, Tennessee, and which circulates in forty-two languages. A retreat leader and teacher of writing, she also serves on the editorial boards of *Pockets* magazine for children, and of *Horizons*, the magazine of Presbyterian women. Her first book, *Breaking and Mending: Divorce and God's Grace* was recently published in the USA.

Rev Dr Colin Morris spent fifteen years as a missionary in Zambia. He is a past President of the Methodist Conference, and was also the minister of Wesley's Chapel in London. Later he was BBC Controller for Northern Ireland. He is a speaker, broadcaster and the author of numerous books.

Rev Richard Ralph has been Principal of Westminster College since September 1996. He taught at Oxford University before serving for seventeen years as Principal of London Contemporary Dance School. He is an Anglican priest in secular employment, retaining active links with a parish in St Leonards-on-Sea, and is a practising dance scholar.

Canon Roger Royle was ordained in the Church of England in 1962 and has held several ministerial posts, including that of Senior Chaplain of Eton College. He is a frequent broadcaster on TV and radio, has presented *Songs of Praise* on BBC One and currently presents *Sunday Half-Hour* and *A Royle Tour* on Radio 2. In 1990 he became Chaplain of the Lord Mayor Treloar College, a school for the physically disabled, and in 1993 he became Chaplain of Southwark Cathedral.

Susan Smith is an editor and proofreader for the Methodist Publishing House. She also writes articles for magazines, mainly about history, and enjoys choral music.

Alison Stedman is a nurse presently working at St Christopher's Hospice in London. She spent more than seven years in the Himalayan kingdom of Bhutan, working for the Leprosy Mission. She has had two anthologies of poetry published: *Faith, Hope, Love* (New Wine Press) and *The Song of the Sparrow* (The Leprosy Mission).

Rev Mark Wakelin spent his early years in Africa, where both his parents were missionaries. A Methodist minister, he has served thirteen years in circuit and three years in the Youth and Community section of the Connexional Team. He is married with three children.

Rt Hon Ann Widdecombe MP was elected Member of Parliament for Maidstone in 1987 and has held a number of Government posts; she was Minister of State at the Department of Employment from 1994-95. In July 1995 she was appointed Minister of State at the Home Office, a position she held until 1997. She is currently MP for Maidstone and the Weald. She is the author of several publications, and has taken part in the BBC's *Any Questions,* as well as various other radio and television programmes. In June 1998 she was made Shadow Health Minister.

Acknowledgements

Methodist Publishing House gratefully acknowledges the use of copyright items. Every effort has been made to trace copyright owners, but where we have been unsuccessful we would welcome information which would enable us to make appropriate acknowledgement in any reprint.

Scripture quotations, unless otherwise stated, are from the New Revised Standard Version of the Bible, copyright 1989 by the Division of Christian Education of the National Council of the Churches of Christ in the USA.

'The Himalayas' by Alison Stedman was originally published in *Faith, Hope, Love* (New Wine Press 1987) and was used again in *The Song of the Sparrow* (The Leprosy Mission 1991).

'The Man' by Edmund Banyard is from the pop cantata *Upside Down and Inside Out,* published by Radius.

'Face to Face with the Messiah' by Michele Guinness is taken from *Child of the Covenant*, first published in 1985 by Hodder and Stoughton, a division of Hodder Headline PLC. Reproduced by permission of Hodder and Stoughton Limited.

Page

13   Rosemary Lindsay, by permission of the author.

23 Kate Compston, from *Encounters*, Prayer Handbook 1988, The United Reformed Church.

25 H. V. Morton, *In the Steps of the Master*, Rich & Cowan Limited.

31 Esther de Waal, Meditations for Jan 17, 20, from *The Upper Room Disciplines 1995*. Copyright © 1994 The Upper Room. Used by permission of Upper Room Books.

34 Gillian Rose, from Network, April 1984. Copyright of the United Society for the Propagation of the Gospel.

45 Dorothy L. Sayers, *The Nine Tailors*, Coronet Books.

45 Edward Rogers, 'Intended to be Used', *Let Us Worship*, Epworth Press.

52 Henry Carter, 'The Place of Methodism in the Church Universal', *The Preacher's Handbook 2*, Epworth Press.

54 Caryll Houselander, *A Rocking Horse Catholic*, Sheed & Ward Limited.

59 'An Anglican Benedictine Abbess', *International Christian Digest*, November 1987.

66 Gordon S. Wakefield, *The Liturgy of St John*, Epworth Press.

68   Flora Slosson Wuellner, 'Gathered in that Name', *Weavings*, July/Aug 1990, The Upper Room.

84   Kenneth G. Greet, *When the Spirit Moves*, Epworth Press.

98   Thomas R. Hawkins, *The Potter and the Clay*. Copyright © 1986 The Upper Room. All rights reserved. Used by permission of Upper Room Books.

98   W. R. Davies, 'The Relevance of John Wesley', *International Christian Digest*, May 1988.

101 Paul Tournier, *The Adventure of Living*, SCM Press 1966.

110 Lorna Lackenby, by permission of the author.

111 Ann Bird, *Spirit Level*, Methodist Publishing House.

112 Denis Vernon, by permission of the author.

121 William Barclay, *The Gospel of Luke*, St Andrew Press.

121 Reuben P. Job, *A Guide to Spiritual Discernment*, comp. Reuben P. Job, and copyright © 1996 by The Upper Room, is used by permission of Upper Room Books.

136 William Portsmouth, *Healing Prayer*, Arthur James Limited.

137   Garfield Wade, 'The Message of Advent', *The Preacher's Handbook 4,* Epworth Press.

139   John Baker, 'Proof of the Existence of God', *London Quarterly & Holborn Review,* October 1962, Epworth Press.

143   *The Observer,* 7th April 1963.

145   P. F. Holland, 'Prayer', *The Preacher's Handbook 3,* Epworth Press.

153   Dorothy H. Farrar, 'The Preacher's Life of Prayer', *The Preacher's Handbook 1,* Epworth Press.

155   Harvey Seifert, *Explorations in Meditation and Contemplation.* Copyright © 1981 The Upper Room. Used by permission of Upper Room Books.

159   Monica Furlong, *Travelling In,* Anthony Shiel Associates Limited.

160-1 Kenneth G. Phifer, *A Book of Uncommon Prayer.* Copyright © 1981 Kenneth G. Phifer. Used by permission of Upper Room Books.